Precision
Putting

Precision Golf
SERIES

JAMES A. FRANK

Editor of *GOLF Magazine*

Human Kinetics

Library of Congress Cataloging-in-Publication Data

Frank, James A.
    Precision putting / by Jim Frank.
      p.   cm.
    Includes index.
    ISBN 0-88011-822-9
    1. Putting (Golf)   I. Title.
GV979.P8F73   1998
796.352'35--dc21

          98-27032
          CIP

ISBN: 0-88011-822-9

Acquisitions Editor: Martin Barnard; **Developmental Editor:** Syd Slobodnik; **Assistant Editors:** Katy Patterson, Leigh LaHood; **Copyeditor:** Don Amerman; **Proofreader:** Jim Burns; **Indexer:** Nancy B. Ball; **Graphic Designer:** Keith Blomberg; **Graphic Artist:** Tara Welsch; **Photo Editor:** Boyd LaFoon; **Cover Designer:** Jack Davis; **Photographer (cover):** Keiichi Sato/Golf Stock; **Photographer (interior):** All photos without credits by Sam Greenwood; Human Kinetics photos by Tom Roberts; **Illustrator:** Keith Blomberg; **Printer:** United Graphics

Human Kinetics books are available at special discounts for bulk purchase. Special editions or book excerpts can also be created to specification. For details, contact the Special Sales Manager at Human Kinetics.

Printed in the United States of America   10 9 8 7 6 5 4 3 2 1

Human Kinetics
Web site: http://www.humankinetics.com/

United States: Human Kinetics
P.O. Box 5076
Champaign, IL 61825-5076
1-800-747-4457
e-mail: humank@hkusa.com

Canada: Human Kinetics
475 Devonshire Road Unit 100
Windsor, ON N8Y 2L5
1-800-465-7301 (in Canada only)
e-mail: humank@hkcanada.com

Europe: Human Kinetics
P.O. Box IW14
Leeds LS16 6TR, United Kingdom
(44) 1132 781708
e-mail: humank@hkeurope.com

Australia: Human Kinetics
57A Price Avenue
Lower Mitcham, South Australia 5062
(088) 277 1555
e-mail: humank@hkaustralia.com

New Zealand: Human Kinetics
P.O. Box 105-231, Auckland 1
(09) 523 3462
e-mail: humank@hknewz.com

To Rich Haskell,
because he introduced me to golf.
And his putting should be as good as the rest of his game.

Contents

Acknowledgments

As much as I might like to think otherwise, there are no unique or original thoughts to be found in this book. Golfers have been putting—rolling a ball toward a hole with a stick—for hundreds, probably thousands of years. And beginning one nanosecond after the first miss, those actions have been subjected to analysis and constructive criticism. That means there was no shortage of great thinkers to borrow from when trying to create a guide to putting. A few have earned special mention.

First, and foremost, is Dave Pelz, unquestionably the leading researcher and teacher of the short game and putting today. As Editor of *GOLF Magazine,* it has been my pleasure to work with Dave for nearly 10 years. In that time, we've written many articles about putting, and I admit to reusing (and rephrasing) many of his ideas here. If after reading this book you want to know more about the physics and deeper details of putting, I strongly recommend Dave's book, *Putt Like the Pros.* It is one of the best books on the subject from any age.

I also was smart enough to steal from my boss, George Peper, who wrote an underappreciated little book of golf instruction back in 1977 called *Scrambling Golf.* His book doesn't only deal with putting, but his thoughts on that subject are clear, cogent, and worth repeating (as I've done here).

Others whose words and works I've consulted in preparing this book include Bobby Jones, Raymond Floyd, Beverly Lewis, Vivien Saunders, Bob Rosburg, and Jim McLean. Also, I've borrowed heavily (often unconsciously) from articles that appeared in *GOLF Magazine.* Thanks to the many editors who worked on them before I did.

Thanks, also, to the models in the photographs: Kristie Seeley and Jim Beasley are teaching pros in the Jacksonville, Florida, area and were great, as was *GOLF Magazine* staff photographer Sam Greenwood, who took the pictures.

To everyone mentioned above and the thousands of others whose ideas have influenced and encouraged golfers over the years, thank you.

Introduction

No golfer, not Jack Nicklaus, not Greg Norman, not even Tiger Woods (well, *maybe* Tiger Woods), expects to hit his drive off the tee and see it roll into the hole. Some players have holed out their second shots, but most simply want to stick the ball close to the flag. If that approach happens to miss the green, the good golfers are trying to hole their pitches, chips, and bunker shots. But, realistically, few do. That's okay; it's expected.

But every golfer expects to hole a putt. Every putt.

And why not? The hole is more than twice as big as the ball, which is rolling on a beautifully manicured carpet of grass, having been hit from a not ridiculous distance away. Ask a non-golfer, and he or she will say that putting looks easy. And, indeed, it does look as if it should be a foregone conclusion: Get on the green, anywhere, and sink the putt. Nothing to it.

© Anthony Neste

Oh yes, there is! Maybe because putting looks so easy (particularly when compared to hitting a long, straight drive or firing a 5 iron in from 180 yards), it proves often ridiculously hard. It has taken the measure of golfers of all skill levels for hundreds of years. It has driven many otherwise happy players from the game. It has taken its toll.

Putting is not easy. A two-footer can have a foot of sideways movement if the green is pitched severely enough (and many are). The ball is rolling on, not flying over, a minefield of hazards between its starting position and the hole: bare patches of more dirt than grass; marks, scrapes, and indentations made by balls hitting the green and golfers too clumsy to lift their feet; the prevailing growth pattern of the grass; the tendency of greens to slope from one side to the other, and sometimes more than one direction at the same time; and, as you'll learn later on, a curious phenomenon called "the lumpy doughnut."

And not only is the green not a level playing field, the golfer faces another obstacle to putting success: himself. Whether it's nerves, complacency, or the demons created by past experiences, any golfer who has played more than a hole or two has had a nasty encounter with a putting green. As soon as the first putt that should have gone in catches

the edge of the hole and spins out rather than dropping, well, that golfer is damaged goods. Who knows when the memories of that miss, or the hundreds to follow, will take over the player's subconscious?

But before giving up on the greens game (and returning this book to the store shelf without buying it), here is a little solace for the golfer's understandably fragile ego. If you look at the statistics (gathered by Dave Pelz, who has made a career of such work), putting truly is harder than you think. What follows is what Pelz calls the "Conversion Chart," the probability that first putts, stroked under tournament conditions by the average PGA Tour pro, find the bottom of the cup. Remember, these are the best players in the world, given one read and one try. Here's how they do:

Distance	Success Rate
5 feet	45-65%
10 feet	15-30%
15 feet	10-22%
20 feet	6-16%
25 feet	4-13%
30 feet	3-9%
35 feet	2-7%
40 feet	1-6%
45 feet	0-5%
50 feet	0-4%

All of which means, if you don't make every putt, you're in good company. True, you should be sinking the short ones with some consistency. But if you're standing outside five feet, you should not expect to make half of them. Get a little farther away and you're talking 1 in 10. So lighten up on yourself.

The other good news about putting is that it is that part of golf most amenable to individuality. You can start from an unusual set-up position or make a strange stroke, but as long as you accelerate the putterhead straight along the target line and have it pointing at your target at impact, you can be a good putter. And as you'll read throughout the following pages, there are many alternatives to try if your method isn't working. There are fundamentals that must be maintained, and I'll point them out; after that, you're on your own and just about anything goes.

Something else about putting: It can be learned. The format of this book is a little theory (what you *should* be doing), followed whenever possible by a drill, a lesson, or an example to help you feel the proper sensation, make the right motion, and experience the satisfaction of success. Putting drills are easy to do, and usually are effective indoors as well as out, so you have no excuse. And many of them actually are fun.

© Sam Greenwood

Let's see. You shouldn't expect to do too well and you can use almost any technique you like. It's easy to learn and can be fun. So what's the problem? You're still going to miss more than you make. Sorry: It's the nature of the beast.

Putting is not easy, but it doesn't have to be hard, either. I hope that if you try some of the methods presented here, you'll experience some success. I can't guarantee you'll never three-putt, or that every putt from 50 feet will find the center of the hole. But you are now in a position to learn the most reliable, time-tested methods. You'll have to practice, but that's to be expected. If you do, your putting and your scores will improve.

© Courtesy of United States Golf Association

The Great Putters
Willie Park Jr.

"The man who can putt is a match for anyone." Those were the words of Willie Park Jr., of Musselburgh, Scotland, son of the first British Open champion, himself the winner of the 1887 and '89 British Opens, and, by all accounts, the first man to recognize the importance of putting.

Before Park's time, putting was almost an afterthought, little more than a way to finish play between long shots. Putting surfaces weren't the hallowed ground they are today: Cups weren't lined until the 1870s, weren't cut to a standard diameter (4.25 inches) until 1891, and the grass received only cursory maintenance until after the turn of the century. But by then, Park, who would practice putting for 12 hours at a time, had shown that a successful short stroke could beat a good long game.

His method was unusual, even for his day. Using a putter he designed, called "Old Pawky," he struck the ball off the toe of the club, and, in Harry Vardon's words, "comes in to the hole from the right-hand side of it." (This deliberate "hooking" of putts might have been a way to produce overspin, which would give the ball a little more momentum, crucial to handling ill-maintained greens. It also was similar to the method employed 60 years later by another great putter, Bobby Locke.) Park also wrote one of the first single-topic golf instruction books, *The Art of Putting* (1920), and popularized the "gooseneck" putter, which had a bent hosel that positioned the clubhead slightly behind the shaft so the hands lead the face into impact. Most putters today have such an "offset" hosel, which encourages a firm stroke.

A perfectionist off the course as well as on, from the 1890s until his death in 1925, Park was a noted golf course designer, responsible for the original layouts of England's Sunningdale and The Maidstone Club on New York's Long Island, and dozens more courses on both sides of the Atlantic.

Chapter 1

The Set-Up

There are a number of essential points to consider for the proper set-up of a putt. These include grip, address, eye focus, alignment, and head movement.

The Grip

Every motion in golf begins with a good grip. This is certainly true in putting, where the placement of the hands on the club has a direct effect on the position of the putterface and the path of the stroke. This is compounded because the putting stroke is relatively short (compared to a full swing) and the target small (only 4.25 inches across). Even slight misdirection as a result of an improper hold can mean a miss, and another putt.

Standard Putting Grip

As stated in the introduction, putting allows for a great deal of individuality. That applies to the grip, and you'll read in this chapter about numerous ways to hold a putter, all of them perfectly legal and, once mastered, very effective. But whichever grip you adopt, it must adhere to certain fundamentals that guarantee the correct relationship between the hands and the club:

1. The palms of both hands should be parallel to each other and parallel to the face of the putter as seen in figure 1.1. That allows you to use the position of the hands to approximate accurately the orientation of the putterface.

1

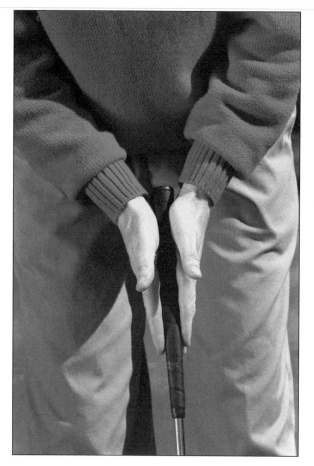

Figure 1.1

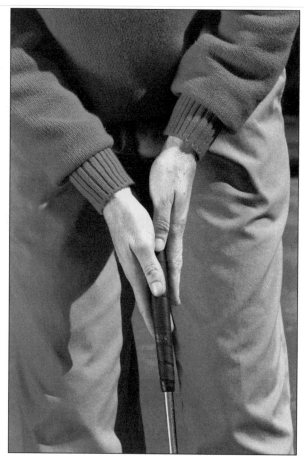

Figure 1.2

2. The thumbs should lay on top of the shaft, not down the sides. See figure 1.2. (Many putter grips, which differ in size and shape from the grips on the other clubs, are flat along the top, making it easier to place the thumbs properly.) This takes the thumbs out of the stroke, giving control to the other fingers and the palms.

3. The palms should press against the sides of the grip, with the fingers wrapping around it, as in figure 1.3. This gives the fingers control of feel and the palms control of power in the stroke.

4. The hands should be linked so they work as a single unit rather than independently and in competition. When the hands fight each other, the stroke is in danger. (The only time the hands are not linked is on a long putter. More on that later.)

Taken together, these fundamentals guarantee there will be little to no manipulation of the putterhead during the stroke, ensuring it can find its way back to the proper impact position naturally.

Reverse-Overlap Putting Grip

For years, the most common putting grip has been the reverse-overlap. It takes its name from the position of the left forefinger, which, for a full

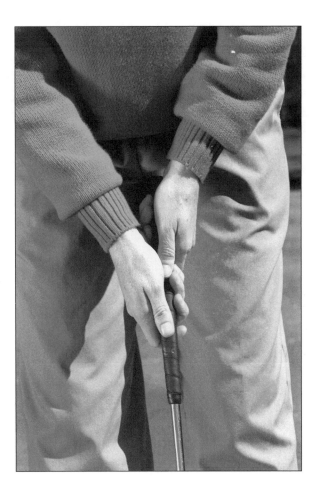

Figure 1.3

swing, usually either intertwines or slides under the right pinkie. But when putting, the left forefinger comes out from under and overlaps the last few fingers of the right hand.

The reverse-overlap has numerous qualities to recommend it. First, with the left forefinger out of the way, all the right fingers are on the handle, providing the utmost in feel. Second, the reverse-overlap promotes keeping the left (leading) wrist firm during the stroke and the putterface square at impact. Third, with the wrists firm, the stroke is controlled by the big muscles of the arms and shoulders rather than the "twitchier" small muscles in the wrists and hands.

1. With the clubface aimed directly at the target, place your right (back) hand lower than the left, their palms parallel to each other and the putterface. Extend both thumbs straight down the top of the shaft (on the flat part of the grip), with the left thumb just tucking under the pad at the heel of the right hand. See figure 1.4a.

2. Wrap the fingers around the grip naturally, being careful to keep the palms parallel. Don't tuck the left forefinger into the right hand, as you do when gripping other clubs. Instead, point the left forefinger toward the ground so it overlaps all the fingers of the

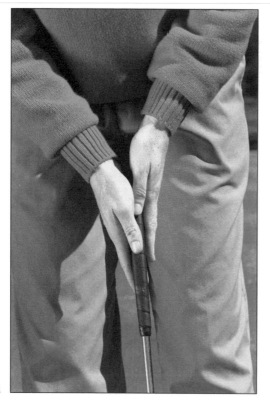 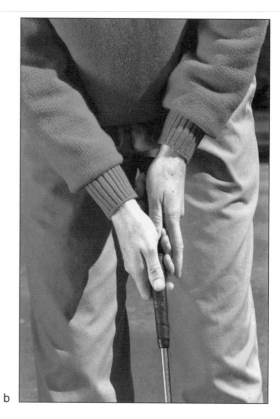

a   b

Figure 1.4

right hand; or let the left forefinger curl more naturally so it rests atop the last two fingers of the right hand. Its position should be a matter of comfort. See figure 1.4b.

When making a putting stroke, there should be almost no sensation in the fingers: They merely hold the putter in position, keeping the face from rotating. Any feeling you have should be in the palms, which are pushing the putter back and through on a straight line perpendicular to the face of the club: That's why the palms must remain parallel to the face.

Be careful about the position of the wrists. If you look at your hands from the side, they should appear arched upward so there is a straight line with no break from the top of the forearms down through the wrists, hands, and puttershaft (figure 1.5). By keeping the wrists straight (which is aided by the upright lie of the putter, the angle that the shaft comes out of the head), it is easier to keep them from hinging during the stroke. Too much wrist action during the stroke leads to inconsistency in direction and accuracy.

Variations in Putting Grips

While the reverse overlap is the most popular grip with both pros and amateurs, it is by no means the only one. Many players have developed unusual grips to combat particular problems—usually too much wrist action—and let them feel comfortable over the ball. But a close look at even the most unusual intertwining of fingers should include the funda-

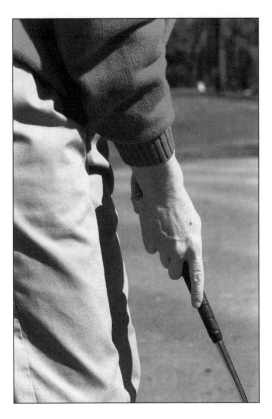

Figure 1.5

mentals explained at the beginning of the chapter, particularly parallel positioning of the palms and the hands linked to form a single, unbreakable unit.

One variation, especially popular among older golfers, is to start with the reverse-overlap grip and then extend the right index finger straight down the side of the shaft, as in figures 1.5 and 1.6. Positioning the forefinger this way makes it easy to place the hands on the grip the same way time after time; it also creates another guide to the direction of the putterface. (Some proponents concentrate on swinging the forefinger as their way of making a smooth stroke.)

Taking a Left-Hand Low Grip

In the last few years, the most popular of the unusual grips has been "left-hand low" (also called, confusingly, cross-handed). Left-hand low reverses the position of the hands from reverse-overlap: The left (forward) hand is below the right (trailing). See figures 1.7a and b. A number of pros, including Fred Couples (figure 1.8), Nick Faldo, and Tom Kite, have putted this way, all of them explaining that it made their left wrist feel firmer and thus less likely to hinge during the stroke. They also reported that the change in grip made it easier to set the putterface square to the target and keep it that way throughout the stroke.

1. Stand square to the target and let your left arm hang straight down until it is below the right (figure 1.7a). You may have to lower your left shoulder slightly.

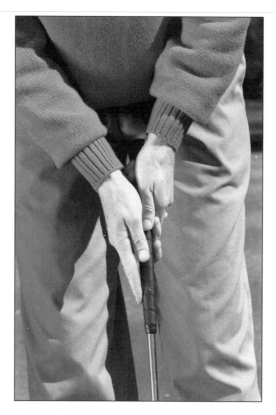

Figure 1.6

a

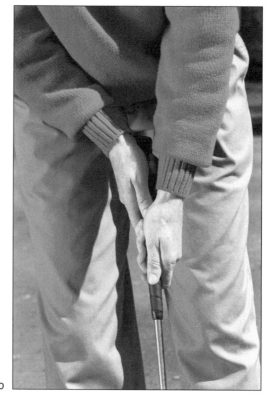

b

Figure 1.7

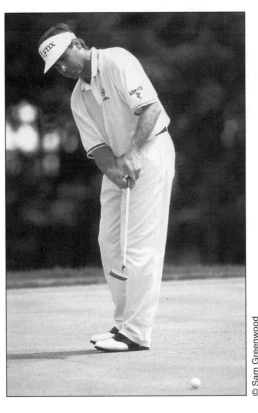

© Sam Greenwood

Figure 1.8

2. Wrap all five fingers of the left hand around the puttergrip. Position the right hand so the thumb presses against the heel pad of the left hand, just below the left wrist. Wrap the right fingers around the grip. Figure 1.7b.

3. Make sure the thumbs are on top of the grip and the palms are on the sides, parallel to each other and the putterface.

It will take a little practice to get used to this grip, but as you do, notice that the left wrist can't break down (hinge), so the putterface maintains its square-to-the-target-line position throughout the stroke. Lowering the left hand also lowers the left shoulder slightly, reducing the tendency to set up in an open stance, the body aimed to the left of the target. Finally, this grip moves the right hand out of the lower "power position": The two hands become more equal, making it easier for them to move as a single unit.

Grip Pressure

In every golf stroke, the body must be capable of moving naturally. One of the great inhibitors of natural movement is tension, which is often caused by squeezing the grip too tightly. In the full swing, tension inhibits releasing the club (the arms rolling over so the clubface returns to square at impact). In putting, too much tension produces stiff, jabbing strokes and bad results.

The first thing to remember about grip pressure in putting is that the hands must squeeze equally: Don't grip tightly with one and loosely with the other or the hands won't work as one. You can get away with too much or too little pressure as long as it is applied equally with both hands.

Unlike the full swing, most instructors like a little more pressure, rather than less, when putting. A little added tension should keep the wrists from breaking down during the stroke. And as stated already, breaking the wrists is a cardinal sin in putting because it destroys consistency.

So take a slightly firmer grip, but not so tight that you can feel the muscles tensing in your arms and upper body. You should be able to feel the grip in your hands as well as a looseness in your forearms. The moment you can see or feel your forearms tighten, you've gone too far.

Practice grip pressure by putting while squeezing the club as tightly as you can, then as lightly as possible. If those are the two extremes—"1" is lightest, "10" is tightest—proper pressure is around 5 or 6. Keep practicing with different amounts of pressure until you feel comfortable and like the results.

Address

The farther you stand from the ball, the more power (and distance) you can generate. That's why you stand farthest from the ball with the driver, closest to the ball with the putter.

Your distance from the ball also is dictated by the club's length and lie angle (the angle that the shaft comes out of the head). The driver is the longest club in the bag, from 43 to 48 inches and sometimes even longer, while the putter is usually the shortest, averaging 34 or 35 inches. Even if you use a long putter, the lie angle is so steep that the clubhead will be only a few inches from your feet. You can get away with this closeness because more than any other shot in golf, the putt isn't about hitting it a long way, but about rolling it a precise distance on a specific line.

So the putter itself helps dictate your stance. (More in chapter 5 about choosing a putter with the correct specifications.) But no matter what kind of putter you prefer, there are a few givens when you have it firmly in your grip and are settling into your posture over the ball:

- There should be a slight bend in your knees, just enough to avoid stiffness and let you stand comfortably.
- The principal point of bending is at the hips (figure 1.9), not the waist. Bending forward from the hips places your head and eyes in the proper position over the ball (see next page) and helps distribute your weight evenly over the feet so you stay in balance throughout the stroke.
- Distributing the weight 50/50 over the feet also helps you make a good stroke, not one that brings the clubhead down too sharply on the ball or catches it on the upswing.
- Your feet should be wide enough apart to form a stable base. For most people, this is about shoulder-width apart (figure 1.10). If your feet are farther apart, your center of gravity is lowered, which may make you feel more secure but may necessitate choking down on the putter or bending the elbows to position the putter. Standing taller, especially for taller golfers, may reduce the feeling of steadiness but can prove helpful if you want to bend your head more over the ball. Experiment with different stances letting comfort, feel, and results be your guide.

Figure 1.9

Figure 1.10

- Your arms should be almost straight (but not stiff) and your hands located directly under your shoulders, as in figure 1.11. If you've bent over enough, that will leave a few inches between your hands and lower body (probably just above the knees), meaning there is sufficient room for the hands to move freely back and forth.

One way to know you're in a good stance is that you'll be able to hold it for a few minutes without feeling tension or pain in your legs, shoulders, and back. Not that you should stay in this position too long, but there will be occasions when you set up over the ball and want to hold your pose comfortably while you turn your head from the ball to the hole and back again to figure how hard you need to stroke the ball. It will help enormously if you can stand there long enough to make that determination without discomfort.

Eyes Over the Ball

The final check that your body is positioned correctly is that your eyes are directly over the ball. They can be slightly ahead or behind the ball, but they still must be over the target line, which extends through the ball to your target. (Behind is better because you'll be able to look up

Figure 1.11

the line to the hole with less twisting of the head. If your head is too far ahead of the ball, it positions your weight forward so you probably will make a more descending blow with the putter.)

When your eyes are directly over the target line, you are set up to make the preferred straight-back, straight-through stroke, keeping the putter directly over the target line for most, if not all, of its path. Some teachers say having the eyes slightly inside the line is okay because that encourages an inside-square-inside stroke (the putter swings inside the line going back, is square at impact, then returns to the inside on the through-stroke), which many pros, such as Ben Crenshaw, use successfully (figure 1.12). But this stroke requires precise contact at the point the putterhead is square; make contact a little early or late and the ball will start to the right or left of your target line. Nobody recommends setting the eyes outside the ball as that leads to an outside-to-outside stroke, by far the least natural and hardest to control.

Here are two ways to check that your eyes are over the ball/target line. The first is simple, something you can and should do often to monitor yourself, not only when your putting has gone bad.

Assume your normal putting stance, setting up to a ball on the green. Once you're in position and comfortable, toss the putter to the side.

The set is at the top.

Staying in your stance, take another ball out of your pocket, hold it against the bridge of your nose, and let go. See figure 1.13. It should hit the ball on the ground or just next to it on either side of the target line. If that happens, your eyes are in the right place. If it hits inside the ball, closer to your body, your eyes are inside the target line, which can lead to pushing putts to the right; if it hits outside the ball, away from your body, your eyes are outside the line and your tendency will be to pull putts to the left.

The second test requires a mirror and a roll of thin, colored adhesive tape. Lay the mirror on the floor and stick a piece of tape down its middle with at least a foot of tape extending off both sides and sticking to the floor. (Use a floor tile or other straight edge to assure accuracy.) Cover the mirror with a piece of paper.

Place a golf ball on the tape just in front of the mirror. Take your putter and get into your stance, aiming at a target farther down the tape. Once in your pose, have someone uncover the mirror.

If your eyes are positioned properly, you'll see your eyelids while your eyeballs will be obscured by the tape. If your eyes are above the tape it means you're leaning too far forward or are too close to the ball at address. Eyes below the tape mean your weight is back on your heels or you're standing too far from the ball. See figure 1.14.

© Anthony Neste

Figure 1.12   **Figure 1.13**

Use the mirror to assume a good stance, standing comfortably with your eyes directly above the tape. Get a feel for the position and practice it every day, using the mirror until you can assume it naturally. (You also can use the tape to help groove a straight stroke, taking the putter back and through while keeping it directly above the strip.)

Alignment

There are three elements to proper alignment in putting: aligning the body, the clubface, and the ball. All three are important if you want consistent results in distance and accuracy.

The ideal body alignment aims all your "pieces"—feet, knees, hips, forearms, and shoulders—parallel to your target line, as in figure 1.15. That makes sense: If you want to make a straight-back, straight-through stroke, set your body parallel to that straight line and you won't have to manipulate your arms or hands to keep the putter on the right path. (It's important to note that the target line is the track you want the ball to begin on, not necessarily a straight line from the ball to the hole. If the putt breaks, curving due to the slope of the green, you must start

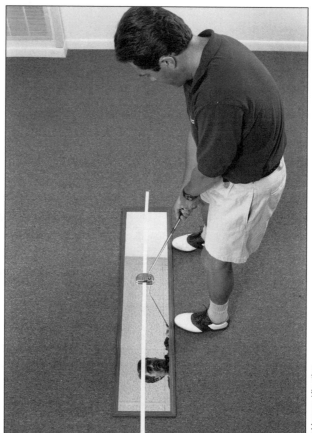

© Human Kinetics

Figure 1.14

Figure 1.15

Figure 1.16

the ball above or below the hole and let it curl back to it. Then your set-up should be parallel to the ball's initial path, its first few inches of roll.)

Some golfers find it more comfortable to set up slightly open to the target line, aiming at least their feet and hips, and sometimes their upper body as well, to the left of the target line (for right-handed golfers). Jack Nicklaus has done this throughout his career, saying it gives him a better view of the green and provides more room for his arms to swing through unimpeded by his body. Despite this set-up, Nicklaus still keeps the putter moving along the target line, not on a line parallel to his open stance (figure 1.16).

Nobody, or at least no good putter, sets up closed to the target line, with any parts of the body aiming to the right of the target line. That would require excessive manipulation to avoid hitting the feet with the putterhead or blocking the movement of the hands with the lower body.

Just as you set your body parallel to the target line, you should begin with your putterface perpendicular to that line (figure 1.17a). And as you make your stroke, keep the putterface perpendicular to the line. (This works on all but the longest strokes, when the club must swing slightly inside going back.) Turning the putterface open (figure 1.17b) or closed (figure 1.17c) to the target line will lead to trouble.

Figure 1.17

How great an effect does clubface alignment have on putting? According to Dave Pelz, 90 percent of the deviation from square is imparted on the ball. Put another way, if the face is open 10 degrees on a 20-foot putt, the ball will miss the hole by three feet to the side.

Ball alignment, where the ball is positioned in the stance, is often overlooked. Lee Trevino once said that one of the most common errors he noticed watching his pro-am partners putt is that they started with the ball too far forward in their stances. While this may have made it easier for them to see, it led to hitting the ball as the putter was on its upswing; as a result, the ball either was lifted off the green or struck with a glancing blow, imparting less than the full power of the stroke on the ball.

Contact should be made at the bottom of the putting stroke, that point where the head is traveling horizontal to the ground. This is usually directly beneath the center of your stance, located in line with your sternum (breastbone), as seen in figure 1.18. However, if your stance is open and you place more weight on your back foot, the low point moves back in the stance, sometimes as far back as off the right (back) heel. If you lean forward, toward your target, the low point moves forward as well, toward your left (front) heel.

Determine your low point by making some practice putting strokes without a ball, noting where the clubhead scuffs the grass: That's the low point and the ball should be placed slightly in front of it.

A little troubleshooting: If your eyes are properly positioned and you're still pushing putts to the right, chances are the ball is behind your low point and should be moved forward in your stance. If you are pulling putts left, the ball is ahead of your low point and should be moved back in your stance.

Head Movement

Not the clubhead, but *your* head: It must remain still throughout the stroke. If your head moves, chances are your body is moving too, and

Figure 1.18

then the putter won't meet the ball where and when it's supposed to. See figures 1.19a and 1.19b for proper head positioning throughout the stroke.

But be careful when keeping the head still. Don't tense the muscles in your neck and shoulders. Don't drop your chin onto your chest and anchor it there. Don't get so stiff in the upper body that you can't make a smooth, rhythmic stroke. Avoid tension.

Rather than thinking about head movement, groove a habit that quietly encourages the head to stay still. For example, watch the putterhead meet the ball and keep looking to see the ground underneath. Or rather than turning your head to watch the ball track to the hole, listen for the sound of it plopping in.

A final point about your head. Nothing ruins a good address position more than getting set over the ball and then lifting the head to take one last look at the hole. Lifting your head lifts your entire body and destroys the perfect putting posture you've established. Instead, once you are set up over the ball, simply swivel your head to the side (figure 1.20), keeping everything else in place, and look from the ball to the hole and back again.

a   b

Figure 1.19

Figure 1.20

© Corbis-Bettmann

The Great Putters
Bobby Jones

The great star of the Roaring 1920s, Bobby Jones didn't so much roar out of the South as he strolled, leisurely and always in control. His record of wins is incredible, and all accomplished as an amateur: four U.S. Opens, three British Opens, five U.S. Amateurs, one British Amateur, and, of course, the "impregnable quadrilateral" (what we now call the "Grand Slam"), when he won all four of the above in a single year, 1930.

As an exemplar of mechanics, Jones is remembered primarily as a ball-striker, using a fluid swing that never varied and was never rushed. It was very much the same on the greens, where he wielded his trademark putter, "Calamity Jane," with a motion as long, loose, and natural as his full swing.

He stood quite tall, with his feet close together, and rather than strike the ball, seemed to sweep the putter through impact. He was among the first to use the same rhythm no matter how long the putt, varying the length of the stroke but never its speed. He must have been a joy to watch.

It's only fair, when talking about Jones, to mention another great putter of that era, Walter Travis. A three-time U.S. Amateur champion (and the first foreign winner of the British Amateur), Travis perfected his green play to overcome the shortness of his long game. Bernard Darwin's description of Travis could easily apply to Jones: "To see him putt was a liberal education in smoothness and rhythm of hitting." And, as Darwin notes, "He [Travis] also must be given some of the credit for another superb putter, for he gave Mr. Bobby Jones a lesson, when that great man had one slightly weak joint in his armour." Among the instruction Travis may have given Jones was to use the reverse-overlap grip: Travis was the first to use this hold, which remains the most popular today.

A final fact about Jones. His long-time weapon, Calamity Jane, carried a tremendous amount of loft, which helped keep the ball high, so it rode on top of the poorly tended greens of his day. After Jones retired from competitive golf in 1930, Calamity Jane was mass-produced and a huge seller for years.

Chapter 2

The Stroke

Putting strokes are like snowflakes: No two are exactly alike. How the golfer stands, grips the putter, and works his body create a unique action back and through.

This individuality is one of the joys of putting. You can get away with a great deal as long as certain basics are present. This chapter will explain those basics, including the path and tempo of the stroke, and explain why it's important to make the same stroke every time. You also will encounter the first of many drills, opportunities to learn, practice, and feel what it's like to putt properly. When you are trying one of the drills, read it through first to be sure you understand it, and then give it a try. If it feels uncomfortable, either you are doing something wrong or your stroke is so wrong that your body is reacting to the correct movements. Don't give up: Keep practicing and it soon will feel normal.

How to Make a Straight Stroke

The first fundamental of consistently good putting is a straight stroke, one in which the putter travels as long as possible directly above the target line back and through. See figure 2.1a–c. Obviously, at some point in a long stroke the putter will have to swing slightly inside; if not, you are manipulating your hands and wrists to keep the putter unnaturally above the line. But for most putts, you can keep the putter directly above the line without any compensating moves.

The most compelling argument in favor of a straight stroke is simple: If the putter is moving along the target line and the ball begins on that line, then the ball is likely to roll along that line.

a

b

c

Figure 2.1

Another reason to employ a straight stroke is its large margin for error. If the club is moving along the target line, then no matter where the ball begins on that line it is likely that the ball will roll straight (if the putterface is square and you make contact close to the sweetspot; more on those variables later). However, if you make an inside-square-inside stroke, your timing must be perfect if you hope to make contact when the putterhead is perpendicular to the target line. Great putters like Ben Crenshaw and Phil Mickelson, who practice for hours a day and get paid for their efforts, have grooved an inside-square-inside stroke and use it with success. Unless you are willing to devote that kind of time to honing and maintaining such a stroke, you are better off with the simpler straight-back, straight-through motion.

The final reason to make a straight stroke is statistical, one of the three factors Dave Pelz identified as crucial to putting success (the first is face angle, described a few pages back). If the putter is not traveling straight down the target line at impact, moving either inside or outside the line, 20 percent of the deviation is transmitted to the roll. So on a 20-foot putt, a putter that is 10 degrees off the target line will send the ball wide by eight inches (that's nearly the width of two holes).

Your ability to make a straight stroke is predicated by your alignment. The putter travels on a line parallel to your shoulders, so it makes sense that you should begin with your shoulders parallel to the target line. Addressing the ball with your shoulders open (pointing left of the target line for right-handed golfers) may feel comfortable, but for many golfers it leads to swinging the putter outside the line going back and across it coming through, creating a glancing blow. Once again, the only way to make a straight stroke from an open-shoulder stance is to unnaturally manipulate your hands, wrists, and forearms, turning them during the stroke to keep the putter on the line. It can be done, but those small compensating moves can easily break down, especially under pressure, which is when you most want to be able to rely on your stroke.

Once your shoulders are parallel to the target line, imagine a line drawn across them and a line running down each arm: Together they form a triangle that should stay intact throughout the stroke. You'll want to remember and use that image later on. The following drill, entitled "Read Between the Lines," deals with a similar situation.

 **Read Between the Lines**

STRATEGY:

To ensure that your ball starts and stays on your intended line, the putter must travel on a straight line back and through, and be traveling directly over the target line at impact.

TECHNIQUE:

There are numerous training aids, called putting tracks, that you can buy to help you practice and groove a straight stroke. These tracks consist of parallel rails, set far enough apart to let your putterhead fit between them and long enough to allow a lengthy stroke.

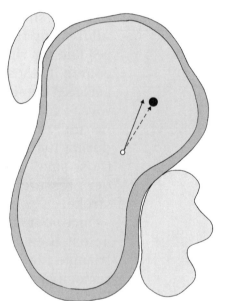

CONCEPT:

Regular practice will train your muscles to take the putter straight back and straight through without banging into the rails.

DRILL:

Putting with the putterhead inside the rails, you'll hit the inside rail if the putter is swinging to the inside, the outside rail if it's swinging to the outside. (If you're hitting the outside rail, you've got a big problem: There is no way to make an outside-square-outside stroke without severe manipulation of the hands and arms, which must be corrected!)

You don't have to buy a putting track: Any straight line will do. You can use string or make a line on the surface of the green with chalk or even white spray paint (but check with the pro first), and practice swinging the putterhead back and forth directly above the line. Or place two 2x4s, or two other golf clubs, side by side and parallel, with room between them for the putterhead.

Read Between the Lines

TIP: Here's how simple it can be. Tie each end of a four-foot-long piece of string to a pencil. Stick the pencils into a putting green so the string is taut and a few inches off the ground, enough so that the putterhead fits beneath. Practice swinging the putter under the string, watching the motion of the head back and forth, keeping it centered under the line. (This is easier if your putter has an aiming line or other mark on the crown: Keep the mark under the string as you swing.) After taking practice strokes without a ball, place one directly under the string and putt it; you may be surprised how far it rolls.

Pendulum Putting Stroke

You may have heard teaching professionals or television announcers talk about a "pendulum stroke" and not understood what they meant. There are a number of ingredients to such a stroke. The first is a consistent rhythm, which is covered on pages 27-29. The second is the triangle formed by the arms and shoulders, which must stay intact throughout the stroke without any hinging of the wrists that would throw the putterhead off line.

The third, to be discussed here, is the swinging of a pendulum around a fixed point. In physics it's called a fulcrum; in putting, this point is the top of your breastbone. If you hold the end of the putter grip lightly against your sternum with one hand and let it swing naturally back and forth, you've created a pendulum. Watch that easy swinging motion in a mirror: It's the kind of stroke you want to make. But because you hold the putter with two hands, which are connected to two shoulders rather than a single point, your pendulum has a slightly different motion. See figure 2.2a-c.

a Address   b Backstroke   c Through stroke

Figure 2.2

Go back to the triangle formed by your arms and shoulders. To make a pendulum putting stroke, rock the shoulders up and down, swinging the triangle back and forth. All the power in your stroke should be provided by that rocking: There is no releasing of the forearms, no hinging of the wrists (figure 2.3), no "hitting" with the hands—all moves that would change the shape of the triangle and change the putterhead's relationship to the hands.

To roll the ball a longer distance, rock the shoulders (or swing the triangle, whichever image you like better) a longer way; for shorter putts, rock them less. Swing the triangle without adding any hand, wrist, or arm motion and you'll develop a smooth, rhythmic pendulum stroke you can depend on.

Feel a Pendulum Stroke

Here's a simple way to feel a pendulum stroke while eliminating any unwanted movement of the hands, wrists, or arms.

Loosely hold your putter in your hands and take your putting stance. Without moving your body, slide the putter up until the top of the grip is touching your breastbone. Regrip wherever your hands fall, somewhere near the putterhead. Keeping the grip against your chest, rock your shoulders back and forth. It should be almost impossible to work any other part of your upper body. This is how a proper pendulum swing feels. See figures 2.4a–c.

Figure 2.3

a

b

c

Figure 2.4

Putting Rhythm

Once you're making a pendulum stroke, the proper rhythm of the stroke should come naturally because the speed of a pendulum is a constant. (Watch a grandfather clock: The pendulum swings at a constant tempo.) That's how it should be in putting: You want to use the same rhythm for all putts, regardless of their length. See figure 2.5.

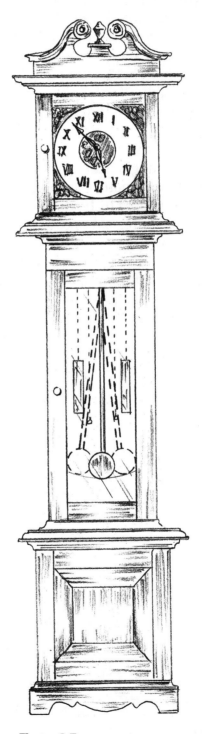

Figure 2.5

That's right: Long putt or short, the tempo or pace of the stroke remains the same! See figures 2.6a and 2.6b. Not only that, but if you make the stroke correctly, the time of the backstroke will be the same as the time of the through-stroke. There should be no rushing coming down, no forcing of the stroke through impact for extra power.

There are many ways to determine your best rhythm. Start by figuring out if you are a quick and intense golfer or one who is slower and more laid back. You want a rhythm that matches your personality.

You can get a good handle on your natural rhythm by measuring the pace you walk on the course. If you walk quickly, you'll do better with a faster putting rhythm. If you walk slowly, a slower, more languid rhythm will do the job. (If you can't easily determine your rhythm, walk side by side with someone you think is fast or slow; you'll quickly get a sense of what you are.)

Once you have a feel for your natural pace, start working with a metronome, finding a beat, *tick-tock, tick-tock*, that appeals to your ear and is easy to coordinate to your stroke. Your rhythm should fall somewhere between 60 and 110 beats per minute; slower golfers will need fewer beats per minute, faster golfers more. What you're looking for is a comfortable tempo, one you can live with and putt to over and over again.

When you know the number of beats that suits you best, make note of it and use the metronome to help you practice: back-through, *tick-tock,*

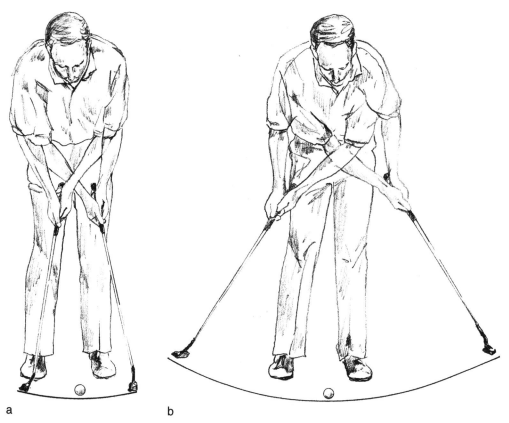

a   b

Figure 2.6

back-through. It won't take long for you to feel the right rhythm for you and your stroke. And should you have putting problems later, knowing your beat count will help you practice and re-establish the right pace.

Always Accelerate

Despite a good stroke and constant rhythm, many golfers commit a cardinal sin on the through-stroke: deceleration. A common sight is a player taking a good, rhythmic backswing and then, sensing that the stroke is too long, trying to slow down on the through-stroke. As a result, the muscles in the arms, hands, and upper body tighten, which kills any feel. The putterhead swings out ahead of the hands and the clubface turns open to the target line. Contact is made with an open face and a tentative stroke, so the ball hops rather than rolls and starts well to the right of the intended line.

The pace of the through-stroke should be the same as the backstroke, but for most golfers that demands consciously accelerating through impact. Concentrating on letting the stroke swing all the way through to its natural, rhythmic finish encourages firmer, more positive contact with the clubface square. An accelerating stroke is essential when putting uphill and on short putts when the idea is to bang the ball to the back of the cup. A firmer stroke also reduces break, and since, as you'll read later, most golfers already underestimate the true break of most putts, acceleration helps cope with a slope. The following drill, "Accelerate Through the Ball," gives you practice with solid aggressive strokes.

2 Accelerate Through the Ball

SITUATION: On medium to long putts the ball stops short of the hole.

STRATEGY:

Learn to hit an aggressive, accelerating stroke. This will ensure more solid contact and increases the likelihood that the putterhead will be square at impact.

TECHNIQUE:

Use your regular putting address and method, but make a conscious effort to "finish" the stroke rather than slowing on the downswing and quitting at impact. Plan to putt "through the ball," and make your finish position at least as long as your backstroke length.

CONCEPT:

Don't try to add "oomph" to a putt by shortening the backstroke and lengthening the through-stroke. This will destroy your natural rhythm and ruin your capacity to correctly judge the amount of stroke needed for the distance.

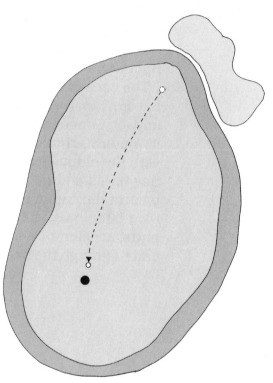

DRILL:

Lay a club down on the putting green so the middle of the shaft is about two inches in front of a hole. Place a ball about two feet on the other side of the shaft and stroke the putt with enough force to make the ball hit the shaft, hop over, and fall into the hole. Use your rhythmic stroke, being sure to swing through just hard enough to pop the ball over the shaft.

Accelerate Through the Ball

TIP: After a few two-footers, do the same at three feet, then four, six, and 10. You will begin to feel an aggressive, accelerating stroke.

Variations in the Stroke

As stated at the beginning of this book, there is no motion in golf that allows for more individuality, or idiosyncrasy, than putting. So although the instruction given so far is sound and sure to help you improve on the greens, there are options you might want to try. One involves the stroke of the putt, the other the pace.

The "Pop" Stroke

Call it a "pop," a "jab," or a "rap," it's a quick stroke made with a short backswing and almost no follow-through. You see it used by a number of well-known tour players, among them Gary Player, Chi Chi Rodriguez (figure 2.7), and Paul Azinger, all of whom probably grew up putting on scruffy, inconsistent greens: They needed to hit the ball with more authority as a way of dealing with the bare spots, unrepaired ball marks, and other imperfect areas between them and the hole.

Although purists want the backstroke and through-stroke equal in length and time, the rap does have qualities to recommend it: It guarantees firm contact and keeps the ball rolling on line, which makes it a good choice for golfers who have trouble with short putts. However, it

Figure 2.7

© Sam Greenwood

is difficult to judge the amount of backstroke needed for longer putts, and if you are trying to groove a rhythmic, same-time-back, same-time-through motion, switching to a rap could have a bad effect on your overall success.

Charge It or Die It?

Should you hit every putt firmly so it bangs into the back of the cup? Or stroke the ball softly enough that it barely falls over the front edge? The choice is yours, and you'll find teachers and tour pros advocating both methods. Furthermore, you may find it makes sense to die the ball in on a downhill putt, when you're worried about rolling too far past the hole, then hit it more firmly on uphill putts to be sure you get it there.

However, for the majority of putts, the best advice comes from Dave Pelz, who performed hours of tests, rolling thousands of balls trying to determine an optimum speed for putting. His studies proved that to handle all the bumps, spike marks, and other variegations on a green (some of which will be described in later chapters), your ball should be rolling at a speed at which, if the hole were covered, the ball would roll right over the top of it and stop 17 inches past (figure 2.8). At this speed, and that's whether you are putting from three feet or 30 (but, obviously, not if you're just a few inches away), the ball is most likely to hold its line all the way to the hole and then not lip out if it catches an edge.

Because golfers are used to putting at a specific target, trying to roll the ball 17 inches past takes practice. Go to a putting green, put down a

Figure 2.8

coin to indicate a hole, and then stick a tee in the ground 17 inches behind it (figure 2.9). Starting from three feet away, see how much harder you have to putt to roll the ball over the coin to the tee. It isn't much. Try it at longer distances, all the way back to 25 or 30 feet. Then try it on breaking putts, uphill and downhill putts, putts of varying distances. Besides increasing your mathematical likelihood of making more putts, grooving a 17-inch-past stroke will have much the same effect as learning to accelerate on the through-swing described above. It will help get the ball to the hole every time!

Make It Routine

Chances are, when you're preparing to hit a full-swing shot, you repeat a series of motions that prepares you to execute. For example, you might start by standing behind the ball and looking from it to the hole, choosing a line of flight. Then you settle in over the ball, waggle once or twice, take a breath, and swing. Whether or not you know it, you've developed a preshot "routine" that you perform to some degree before most of your shots.

Figure 2.9

A preshot routine gets you ready mentally and physically to make your best possible swing. It tells your mind that it's time to get into the swinging mode, shutting out all distractions, focusing in on the ball and the conditions, and allowing the swing you've spent hours grooving on the range to take over.

The same should be true when putting. Once you've determined your line and given some thought to the necessary speed, you should go through a prestroke routine—the same series of motions every time, culminating with your stroke. Ingraining a prestroke or preshot routine stops you from thinking about the physical part of the motion, which you should have developed on the range or practice green. The routine tells you it's time to let your subconscious take over and make that good full swing or putting stroke.

There is not one prestroke routine perfect for all golfers. It takes experimentation to find the one that works for you, letting you get comfortable and ready to putt. But among the elements you should consider for your routine are one or two looks at the hole and some sort of trigger just before starting the stroke: It could be a slight forward movement of the hands, a last glance toward the hole, anything that flips the switch to "automatic pilot" for the stroke and lets it begin smoothly rather than with a jerk or jolt.

Your entire prestroke routine shouldn't take more than a few seconds. Remember, you've already established line and speed: The routine simply takes you from finishing your address to making the stroke, and when done properly, and rehearsed with every practice stroke you make, it will clear your mind and clear the way for the perfect putting motion time and again. The next drill helps you "Develop a Routine."

3 Develop a Routine

SITUATION: Your putts are inconsistent. What was an easy six-footer on the front nine turns into a three-putt on the back.

STRATEGY:

Develop a preshot routine before every putt. This will help to eliminate tension, build confidence, and get your body set to make a good stroke without being distracted by mechanics.

TECHNIQUE:

Set up as you would over every other putt, square to your target line and ready to go. Don't change your grip pressure or any other tension-producing element of your set-up.

CONCEPT:

Make practice putts while consciously changing your last three to five motions before making each stroke. You'll see how a consistent, comfortable routine encourages consistent, good strokes, and good results.

DRILL:

Before beginning the stroke, turn your head once, twice, then three times to look at the hole, varying the number of looks before each putt. Lift the putterhead off the ground, forward press the hands toward the hole, take a breath, do different little things without changing your address position immediately before swinging the putterhead away from the ball. Every different series of motions will produce different results.

Now try the same series of motions a few times in a row. After just three or four putts, you should begin to notice that the stroke comes more naturally, the result of the motions that preceded it. The more these motions are ingrained, the easier it is to forget about mechanics and just let the stroke happen.

TIP: It will take some experimentation, but you should quickly find the two to three movements you need to incorporate into your prestroke routine. They will differ for every golfer, so *don't* copy someone else's routine. In fact, once you have a routine (which you must use in practice to ingrain), don't watch other golfers use theirs if you're likely to want to copy it.

Putt to an Intermediate Spot

You've squatted behind the ball and seen the line to the hole. You stand up, settle into your address position, then turn your head trying to find that perfect line again. What happened to it? Where did it go? It's still there; it's just harder to see.

Because your head is over the ball and turned, positioning the eyes one above the other rather than side by side as we're used to, it's very hard to keep track of your target line. So rather than looking for the line, look for a spot, a point just a few inches ahead of the ball that you'll have no trouble seeing both from behind the ball and standing over it. It can be an old ball mark, a slight discoloration, anything you can notice without having to alter any part of your address. See figure 2.10.

Besides being easier to see, an intermediate spot takes pressure off your putting. Rather than trying to find the hole, think about rolling the ball over your spot at the right speed. You'll stop worrying about results and begin thinking "line" and "length." You'll find it easier to make a good stroke when you're concentrating on the first few inches of the roll and not the entire distance.

Figure 2.10

© UPI/Corbis-Bettmann

The Great Putters
Bobby Locke

Arthur D'Arcy "Bobby" Locke is one of those great international players almost unknown to American golf fans. A star in his native South Africa, he won that country's Open and Amateur titles by the age of 18. He turned pro in 1938, at 21, and, looking for better competition, took his game on the road, winning a host of other nations' championships. In 1946, he tied for second at the British Open and, in one of the most lopsided results of all time, went head to head with Sam Snead in a 16-match series throughout South Africa, winning 12 and losing only two.

His secret was hitting from right to left, eking out every yard by playing a big hook. But his greatest strength was on the greens, where he also played to hook. Or so it seemed.

Locke went against nearly every accepted precept of good putting. After a long time judging the putt, his purposeful prestroke routine never varied. He positioned the ball well forward, off the big toe of his left foot. He took a closed stance, pulling his right foot well off the target line, so he was aligned well right of his target. His putter traveled straight back and through along the same right-aiming line, but because the ball was so far forward, at contact the clubhead was square to the target.

Due to the closed stance and path of the clubhead, his putter seemed to swing back to the inside after contact. This imparted topspin on the ball, which meant he didn't need a big, hard stroke to hit it a long way. Not surprisingly, he was a wonderful lag putter.

But he did not hook his putts: It just looked that way. Like all great putters, his clubhead was square to the target and traveling on the target line at the moment of impact.

He brought this unusual game to the United States in 1947, when he won six events and finished second on the money list. He won three tournaments in each of the next two years, but this success, plus, perhaps, his deliberate nature, upset his rivals. To appease some American players, the PGA banned Locke, citing a flimsy excuse about ignoring commitments.

The tour later lifted the ban and apologized, but Locke never forgave. He played most of the rest of his career in Europe, winning the British Open four times, in 1949, '50, '52, and '57. He retired in the late '50s with more than 80 worldwide wins.

Chapter 3

Situations

The previous chapter began with the statement that no two putting strokes are alike. The same is true of putts. Play golf for 100 years and, except for the tap-ins, you'll likely never encounter two putts that play exactly the same.

They will vary in distance, and a two-foot putt is not the same as a three-footer when it comes to how hard you have to hit it. The same is true of a 22-foot putt and a 23-footer: The difference might not be great, but there is a difference. Then there are variations in the green surface, uphill, downhill, side slopes, and tiers. All affect how the putt is played.

These situations must be dealt with on every putt. You must know how to judge distances and change your stroke accordingly. What are the tendencies on a two-tiered putt? How much faster will a downhiller roll? Should a sloping putt be hit harder to minimize the break or softer to maximize it?

These are all situations that can be learned only two ways: practice and experience. This chapter aims to provide a little of both.

Judging Distance

Putting has two components: accuracy and distance (or, if you prefer, line and length). The keys to accuracy are a good stroke made with the face angle square to the line at impact, while distance is determined by the length and force of the stroke. These have been covered in the previous chapter on the putting stroke. The following drills help you judge distances.

4 Feel the Speed

SITUATION: You have a hard time developing a sense of how hard to hit the ball on putts longer than two or three feet.

STRATEGY:

Your feel for distance will change every day, and is affected by the speed of the greens. You need to get a feel for your stroke and the greens before beginning play.

CONCEPT:

Making a few practice putts before the round is always a good idea, but hitting to a hole forces you to think too much about results and not enough about technique and feel.

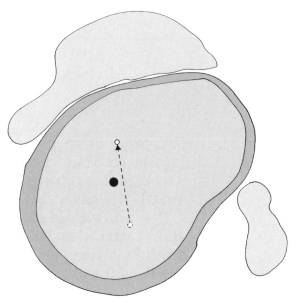

DRILL:

Drop five or six balls on the practice green and putt one of them to a spot (*not* a hole) about 10 feet away. Putt the other balls to the first one, trying to cozy them close. After doing this to 10 feet, do the same to a spot 20 feet away. Then five feet, then 30.

TIP: Hit only five or six balls to each spot. If you roll too many, you'll get stuck at that distance in your mind. Finish with a short distance and be sure to accelerate and use your routine on every putt.

After that, your best source of distance control is experience. As you play more and, using a good stroke, see how putts roll and react on different greens, you'll begin developing a feel for how long a stroke produces how long a putt. If you change putters or the type and make of ball you regularly use, your feel will have to change as well. As with everything else in golf, don't make any changes without spending some time in practice to gauge the effect of your new equipment.

Between the Strings

5

> **SITUATION:** Your distance control is erratic. You're not hitting your first putts close enough to assure tap-ins.

STRATEGY:

You need to be able to hit a specific target surrounding the hole. An inch or two difference on the length of a putt can make the difference between holing out and missing.

CONCEPT:

Precise distance control, even on relatively short putts, is crucial to scoring.

DRILL:

Lay two pieces of string, each about two feet long, on the practice green (not near a hole). They should be parallel to each other and about 12 inches apart. Starting from a few feet away, stroke four or five balls so they finish between the pieces of string. Once you can stop all the balls between the strings, move them six inches apart and roll the balls again.

Between the Strings

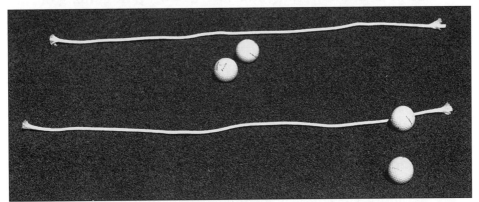

TIP: Also vary the length of the putt, but as you get farther from the strings, give yourself a larger margin for error. Also, never leave a ball short of the closer string; if you do, start all over.

When you go out to play a round of golf, the speed of the green is a variable, changing every day and at every course, which means the distance your putts roll will be affected. You have to learn to judge the distance of a putt and combine that with the green speed to have a chance of rolling the ball into the hole.

Your first place to look for help is the practice green. You should make at least a few short putts and a few long putts before beginning play so you get a feel for your stroke that day.

The practice green also can help you judge, although not always with great confidence, the speed of the greens on the course. Theoretically, the practice green should roll at the same speed as the 18 greens you'll soon encounter, but it often doesn't because of the heavy traffic it gets and the fact that it's usually in an open, exposed area (where it is more susceptible to the weather). If you have any doubts about the speed, ask someone in the pro shop if the practice green is a good indication of what's in store on the course.

Uphill Putts

Putting uphill actually works in the golfer's favor by encouraging a firmer stroke. The ball must be hit a little harder because it's running up a slope. Furthermore, because the hole is slightly higher in the back than the front, the back lip becomes a backstop.

"Charging the hole" has other advantages. By stroking the ball a little harder, you can play less break (a green's side slope), and it's easier to hit a firm putt straight than trying to curl it with any accuracy. Also, should you miss, the uphill will keep the ball from rolling too far past the hole; at the worst, you'll face a short putt coming back, one you've already seen roll past the hole so you'll know how it will move. (Be sure to watch how the ball rolls past. That means if you miss, don't turn away in disgust until *after* the ball has stopped rolling.)

On uphill putts, be careful not to get overzealous and let your head and body move during the stroke. Use your same smooth, rhythmic stroke; just make a longer back- and through-swing as a way of generating the extra power you need.

You want to hit the ball firmly, to the back of the hole (remember the 17-inch rule), rather than trying to die it in over the front edge. So practice making the ball hit the back of the cup before it finds the bottom. See figure 3.1. This is an especially effective drill on a flat practice green.

If your body wants to get into the stroke, widen your stance slightly and keep your eyes fixed on the ball until after impact. Don't add tension to the upper body, but think about maintaining a steady head and letting the rocking of the shoulders create the stroke.

Finally, try gripping higher on the club, closer to the end. This effectively lengthens your putter, so the same stroke will produce more power.

Just remember to stand a little taller and make practice strokes first so you don't scuff the ground, which will alter the face angle coming into the ball. The next drill "Aim for the Tee," will help your uphill-putt stategy.

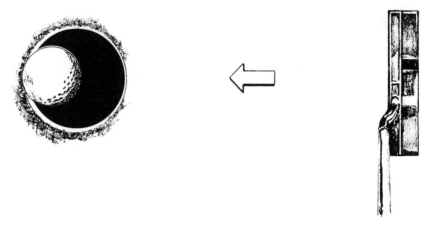

Figure 3.1

6 Aim for the Tee

> **SITUATION:** You have a hard time judging the speed of the greens, and often leave your uphill putts short.

STRATEGY:

When the uphill slope of the green is likely to affect the roll, you must make a slightly longer, "harder" stroke to be sure of getting the ball to the hole.

TECHNIQUE:

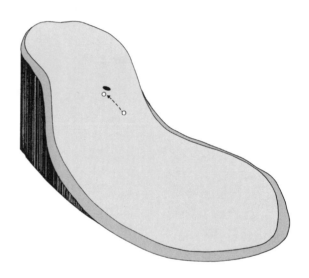

In this situation you should target the back of the hole, not the front edge or the center. By aiming for the back of the hole, you are encouraged to hit the ball a little firmer, which will make sure you get it there.

CONCEPT:

There are two reasons to love uphill putts: 1) It's easier to make a firmer stroke than a softer one; and 2) the back of the hole is slightly higher than the front, creating a "backstop" that will keep your ball from rolling past.

DRILL:

On the practice green, find an uphill putt to a hole. Stick a tee about 1/2-inch directly behind the hole. Make practice putts with the tee as your target. The balls should "clank" the back of the cup and drop in.

Aim for the Tee

6

> **TIP:** Don't set the tee too far behind the hole or the ball will be traveling too fast and hop over the back of the hole. When you face an uphill putt on the course, imagine a tee just behind the back of the hole and make it your target.

Downhill Putts

Downhillers are many golfers' nightmare. They can't seem to make a stroke that hits the ball softly enough that it just topples into the hole. More commonly, they decelerate on the through-stroke, tighten their muscles, and open the clubface, starting the ball off-line; it might catch a lip but spins out violently, and because it's downhill, it rolls too far away to be a tap-in. (Television announcers refer to this jokingly as a "power lip-out." They can laugh; they're in the booth.)

On a downhill putt, the back of the hole is lower than the front so there is no backstop, which means the ball can easily fly over the hole if it's going even a little too quickly. Here are two ways to handle downhillers.

The first and most commonly taught method is to strike the ball off the toe of the putter (figure 3.2a–b). By hitting away from the sweetspot,

a

b

Figure 3.2

less force is applied at impact and the ball rolls more slowly. But when the putter encounters something at the toe, the heel of the club juts forward, opening the clubface and pushing putts to the right. If you are going to hit downhillers this way, grip the putter a little more tightly to keep the face from opening.

You might find it easier and more effective to choke down on the putter, sometimes actually gripping the shaft. Choking down effectively shortens a club, so less force is applied at impact (figure 3.3). (It's also very difficult to make a long backswing when you're bent over.) On severe downhill putts, don't be afraid to grip way down the club, placing your hands just above the clubhead if necessary. It will be difficult to make a natural stroke, but it can be done with practice. Then you'll see that it is easy to hit even a fast downhill putt a short, controllable distance.

Because a downhill putt rolls slowly, its break will be exaggerated. Aim higher than you normally would for the sideways movement. And whatever you do, *do not* hit the ball harder as a way of reducing the amount of break; it won't reduce break, and you'll be standing over a very long come-back putt.

But take heart. If you do miss, the putt coming back is almost certain to be uphill, which means you can catch your breath, set up normally, and be a little more aggressive. The next drill will help you avoid the long come-back putt.

Figure 3.3

7 Leave It Short

SITUATION: Tricky downhill putts give you fits. If you don't sink it, your ball runs well past the hole leaving you with a long second putt back up the hill.

STRATEGY:

The hardest thing about a downhill putt is making a soft stroke that also is a good stroke. This should convince you it can be done, but it does take practice.

TECHNIQUE:

The set-up for a downhiller is a matter of choice. As explained in the text, you can use your regular address and play the ball off the toe of the putter (be sure to grip extra firmly but without creating tension in the arms and upper body), or choke well down the shaft. Either of these will work with the drill: In fact, try them both with the drill and use it to help you decide which method is better for you.

CONCEPT:

Very simply, if you can leave a downhill putt short of the hole, you've got great control. You'll also develop the confidence that it can be done. But remember, you're more likely to be relaxed and in good physical control on the practice green than you are on the course. So the same stroke that leaves it short in practice may have some unconscious extra "oomph" to it during play.

DRILL:

Find a downhill putt on the practice green of at least three feet and putt balls at the hole trying to stop them an inch or two above the hole. If your green offers a variety of slopes, keep moving around until you find one so steep that it's all but impossible to stop a ball short of the hole. Make the softest stroke possible and see how far past the ball will roll. Try to remember that extreme and think about it on the course when you face another, yet less steep, downhill putt. Have confidence that you can make the real one.

Drill

Tip

TIP: Once you've mastered stopping the ball short of the hole, lay two clubs on the green, about five inches apart, leading to the hole. Beginning at the other end of the clubs, make downhill putts that not only stop short of the hole but roll perfectly straight, end over end. Once you can do that, you've developed terrific downhill control.

Long Putts

Simply because your ball is on the green doesn't mean you should expect to drop the first putt. The "Conversion Chart," included in the introduction, proves that it is unlikely long putts will go in. So somewhere between 20 and 30 feet, depending on your skills, you should stop thinking about holing out and concentrate on rolling the ball close enough to ensure a tap-in two-putt. The statistics are strongly against you holing a bomb; when you do, it's as much luck as it is your good stroke and aim. So take some pressure off by playing to get down in two. (It might ease your mind to know that the concept of par is getting your ball on the green "in regulation"—in one shot on a par-three hole, two on a par-four, three on a par-five—and taking two putts to get down.)

But if two putts are sufficient from long range, any more than two are wasted. Learn to "lag" the ball so close with the first putt that the second becomes a no-brainer.

On long putts, most golfers have no trouble controlling direction—reading the break and keeping the ball on line. Where the trouble comes is with length, leaving the ball well short or running it well past the hole. Don't waste a lot of time figuring out how much the ball is going to move side to side: Take a quick read, find your line, and then concentrate on distance.

Start by shooting for a realistic target. The hole is only 4-1/4 inches across, so it's almost impossible to see when you're 30, 40, or 50 feet away. Rather than aiming at it, plan to lag the ball into an imaginary six-foot circle around the hole, as in drill #8 photos (page 59). That way you'll face nothing longer than a three-foot second putt.

Check the surface. You don't have to walk the entire way to the hole to realize that the putt is mostly uphill, downhill, or sidehill. Once you've characterized the terrain, take enough practice strokes that you feel comfortable.

When checking the overall slope of the green, worry more about the slope in the second half of the putt, as it nears the hole. When it leaves the putterface, the ball will have enough steam to handle most of the early break without effect; it's only as it slows down toward the hole that sideslope will come into play.

Try to make the same good, rhythmic stroke you'd make on a six-footer. The only difference is, the stroke will be much longer, probably even swinging to the inside on the backswing and the follow-through. Be prepared for that and for generating a little lower-body motion; it's almost impossible to avoid on long putts, and if you try to stop it, you'll add tension. So let yourself make a big, and natural, swing. See figures 3.4a and 3.4b.

Long putt drills entitled "Knock It Close" and "Close Your Eyes" can be found on pages 58-59 and 60-61.

a

b

Figure 3.4

The "Chiputt"

Many golfers have trouble with long putts because the stroke is longer than they can handle comfortably, their putting crouch doesn't provide a good view of the hole, and they can't figure the distance. That's why Dave Pelz came up with an easy alternative he calls the "chiputt," which mixes the best qualities of the chip and putt.

Conventional chipping technique calls for standing tall, almost straight up, which makes it easy to see the hole, get a good sense of the line, and make a smooth, long swing that propels the ball an accurate distance. The chiputt also begins with a tall stance. And chip shots are played from back in your stance, so the ball comes off the club low and with power; doing the same with the chiputt makes it easier to roll the ball a long way.

Start by holding your putter with whatever grip you use when chipping. Stand tall—no putting crouch here—with feet together and stance slightly open (aiming left of the hole). Play the ball midway between the ankles; because your feet are close together, that's back in your stance, behind your breastbone. Make a long, rhythmic stroke, your hands leading the clubhead into the ball. See figures 3.5a-c. On very long putts you may want to let the lower body turn a bit to maintain a natural rhythm.

Practice the chiputt before trying it on the course; with a little work it will prove very effective. It's also a great shot when you are well off the green and there's nothing but short grass, fairway, and putting surface between you and the hole.

a

b

c

Figure 3.5

8 Knock It Close

SITUATION: On putts of 30 feet or more, you find it very difficult to get close enough so you can get down in two.

STRATEGY:

Long putts aren't supposed to go in; when they do, it's as much luck as your skill. But you are supposed to leave long putts close enough to the hole that your second putt is a gimme.

TECHNIQUE:

Envision a six-foot circle around the hole. Check the surface of the green, paying more attention to the second half of the putt, as it nears the hole. Pick your aiming point and make the same good, rhythmic stroke you'd make on a six-footer, just longer.

CONCEPT:

By trying to finish inside the six-foot-wide circle, you eliminate mental pressure and physical tension. You're not supposed to make it, so don't be upset when you don't. Practice this attitude on the putting green, and keep it with you in play: You'll find your stroke is smoother than if you were expecting to hole out, which could result in a few unexpectedly dropping in!

DRILL:

Use tees or a piece of string to mark the six-foot circle around a hole on the practice green. Starting at 30 feet away, putt three or four balls so they finish inside this circle. If you finish long or short of the circle, start all over again. Alternate distances, jumping from 30 to 50, then back to 40, 25, 55, and so on.

TIP: Don't spend too much time on long putts. Chances are you won't face too many during a round, and you don't want to have "get it close" imprinted on your brain when facing a 10-footer that you should be trying to make.

9 Close Your Eyes

SITUATION: Your long putts are erratic, and sometimes roll way off your intended line.

STRATEGY:

On very long putts, hand-eye coordination is disturbed because the length of the stroke has to be so long. The eyes can't process the distance properly, which leads to an uncertain stroke by the arms.

TECHNIQUE:

As in the "Knock It Close" drill on page 58, place a six-foot circle of string or tees around the hole and set up at least 30 feet from the hole. You're still trying to finish inside the circle, making a good stroke. The only difference is, once you've looked at the target for the last time, turn your head back to look at the ball and then close your eyes.

CONCEPT:

Taking away vision forces you to develop good long-range touch and lets the arms make a freer stroke. It also lets the body participate in the motion naturally.

DRILL:

Alternate long putts with the eyes open and closed and check the results. Again, alternate distances, but also alternate which method you use first, eyes open or eyes closed.

Close Your Eyes

TIP: Putt with your eyes closed on the course. If it eliminates tension in practice, how do you think it will do in real play? That's right: There's more at stake, therefore more anxiety, when you're playing for score or money. Whatever you can do to relax makes sense. And, as stated above, try it on shorter putts, too (especially on short ones and uphillers, whenever you want to make a slightly more aggressive stroke).

Short Putts

"A good many short putts are missed through nothing less than rank carelessness," wrote Bobby Jones back in the 1920s. "The thing looks so simple that it is hard to view it seriously."

What was true in the Roaring '20s, when golf was played in ties and knickers and with hickory-shafted clubs, remains true today. The short putt can be a killer. Never take a short putt for granted or change your technique: Go through your routine, get comfortable, and make a good stroke.

For most short putts, anything inside about five feet, the best advice is to hit the ball firmly. Stroke the ball a little harder than you think necessary, playing for the back of the cup. See figure 3.6. This way you can eliminate some or all of the break, and, as noted above, it's always easier to deal with a straight putt than one that curves. (However, if the sideslope is severe, you might want to play it more delicately, as described in the "downhill putt" section.)

Figure 3.6

One way to be sure of making a firm stroke is to concentrate on the follow-through. Strive for a slightly longer than normal finish, holding it, and keeping your head still, until you hear the ball plop into the hole.

Finally, develop short-putt confidence by holing them all. In weekend play, many golfers concede the little ones to their partners and opponents. While a gentlemanly gesture, it actually weakens your nerve, which will be tested if you ever play competitively, when every ball must be putted out. So even when the short ones are conceded, play them. (Walter Hagen, another star of the '20s, used to concede short putts early in a match, giving his opponent a false sense of confidence. But over the final holes, Hagen would demand that everything be putted out. His opponent suddenly had to start grinding on putts he'd taken for granted. Not very nice, but it proves the point.) The following drill, "Circle the Hole," helps you overcome short-putt problems.

10 Circle the Hole

SITUATION: You aren't making the short putts, those under six feet, that are so crucial to good scoring.

STRATEGY:

You need two things to be a good short-putter: 1) A good, consistent stroke; and 2) confidence. You should have been working on the first all along. This drill will help develop the second. If you don't believe it, watch the pros: They do this drill all the time.

TECHNIQUE:

There are no tricks, no gimmicks, for holing the short ones. In fact, because the distance is so short, it puts extra pressure on making a firm, straight-back, straight-through stroke. You usually want to make an aggressive stroke and play a little less break—all the more reason to be sure your ball will roll straight.

CONCEPT:

Once again, you can't go wrong on the practice green by hitting the back of the cup with the ball. You'll develop a firm, confident stroke.

DRILL:

Place eight to 10 balls in a circle around the hole, starting about two feet away. Stand over each ball, go through your routine, and knock them in, one after another. If you miss one, start over again. After holing them all, move out to three feet and do the same thing. Then four feet, five feet, and so on. This helps groove a firm stroke and, because the green probably is not flat on all sides, offers a good test of how the ball reacts to break from various short distances.

Circle the Hole  **10**

Drill

Tip

TIP: Once you've mastered the circle of balls, give Greg Norman's short-putt test a try. Claiming it helps hone his nerves as much as his stroke, Norman tries to hole 25 two-footers in a row. Once he's done that, it's 25 three-footers. Then, depending on the time (and his success to that point), he attempts four- and five-footers. He claims to end every practice session this way, and it has made him one of the best putters on the tour.

Breaking Putts

Believe it or not, you rarely encounter a perfectly flat green. Why? Because putting surfaces are sloped in order to let water drain off. But just as inclines let raindrops roll away, they also cause rolling balls to curl off-line. You must learn how to deal with the effect this sloping will have on your putts.

We've already discussed uphill and downhill putts, which also result from tilting turf. But what do you do when the slope runs from left to right or right to left, meaning the ball wants to move sideways during its journey to the hole? How well you read and play the slope, called "break," is key to your putting success.

Reading a green means figuring out how, and how much, the putt will curl. Your reading routine should start before you reach the green: Begin looking as you walk up the fairway, judging the overall slope of the land and noting any geographic features (hills, valleys, bodies of water) that will come into play. Once you've reached your ball, form a fast impression of what you think it's going to do. Then spend a few seconds looking from the ball to the hole and, if necessary, from the hole back to the ball, finalizing your impression. Do your reading quickly, while other players are setting up and stroking their putts, so you're set to go when it's your turn.

Once you know how a putt will break, start thinking about how much. Will it move from right to left six inches or two? Experience is the best teacher, and you'll learn as you play how to judge. Obviously a steep slope creates more break than a shallow one. But there are other factors to consider. The following chart explains some of the conditions that tend to exaggerate or minimize break. The drill after that, "Hit It Straight," gives you practice at sinking breaking putts.

PLAY MORE BREAK . . .	**PLAY LESS BREAK . . .**
1. When the green is hard, so the putt rolls faster.	1. When the green is soft, and therefore slower.
2. When the green is dry, which also makes the ball roll faster.	2. When the green is wet. (However, early-morning dew actually can make a putt roll faster, the ball skidding across the thin wet layer like a hydroplaning car.)
3. When the grass is growing in the same direction as the slope. (This is called "grain" and will be discussed in a later chapter.)	3. When the grain is growing into, rather than with, the slope.
4. When the wind is blowing in the same direction as the slope.	4. When the wind is blowing into, rather than with, the slope, or when there is a strong headwind.
5. When the putt is running downhill, increasing its speed.	5. When the putt is also uphill, decreasing its speed.
6. On greens of Bermuda or other bristly, warm-weather grasses (discussed in a later chapter).	6. On greens of bent or other lusher, longer, cool-weather grasses.
7. In the morning (after greens have been freshly mown for the day).	7. In the afternoon, since the grass has been growing all day.

11 Hit It Straight

SITUATION: You have trouble sinking breaking putts or tend to hit through the break and well past the hole.

STRATEGY:

Every putt is a straight putt. Even if the putt breaks, you always want to make a straight stroke toward the target. On a breaking putt, your target becomes a spot somewhere to the side of the hole: Aim it there, make a straight stroke, and let the contour of the land move it to the hole.

TECHNIQUE:

Don't set up to the side and then "steer" the putt to the hole. Read the green, pick your target, then putt it there at the right speed. (On a breaking putt, don't even think about the hole or you might subconsciously steer it in that direction. Your spot becomes the "hole.")

Some players don't like to play break, so they hit the ball harder than normal, trying to minimize the slope's influence. The problem is, a hard-hit putt that misses will roll well past the hole. Play a breaking putt harder only when it is also short and uphill, when you want to be sure of getting it to the hole.

CONCEPT:

When you know the putt will break, it's hard to think of it as straight. But you must ingrain a straight stroke or you'll never consistently make the right putt for the break. Only by grooving a straight stroke in all situations will your putting improve.

DRILL:

Find a breaking putt on the practice green and, however you can, determine its break. Once you know how the ball will move, set up to make the putt, using any of the straight-putt practice methods described in chapter 2 on "The Stroke" (see "How to Make a

Straight Stroke," p. 19)—a putting track, two pieces of wood (below), a string between two pencils, a line drawn on the green—to help you make a straight-back, straight-through stroke. With one of these devices, make a straight stroke and see how the ball bends. Don't worry too much about the results; you can change your read (more on that on page 76) and re-aim. Just be sure to keep making a straight stroke.

TIP: Another common, almost subconscious, correction golfers make is to change their stance on breaking putts. When the putt slopes left to right, they open their stance to be sure the ball starts a little higher. On right-to-left breakers, they close their stance. These compensating moves tend to come after experience has told them that they aren't playing enough break. They'd be better off simply aiming farther away from the hole and making a good, straight stroke.

The "Pro Side"

The high side of the cup, above the hole on a breaking putt, is called the "pro side" because that's where the pros usually miss. The side below the hole is the amateur side because that's where most amateurs miss. The reason is simple: Amateurs read too little break and then steer the ball back to the hole. The pros want to give the ball a chance to go in, which means keeping it above the hole as long as possible. See figure 3.7. The following drill, "Hit It High," guides you to sink those breaking putts.

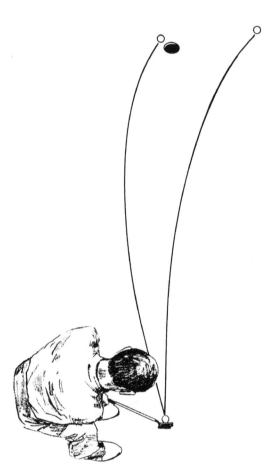

Figure 3.7

12 Hit It High

STRATEGY:

There are two ways to miss a breaking putt, above the hole and below the hole. If you miss below the hole, the ball never had a chance to go in; it was never hit high enough. But if you miss above the hole, it at least had a chance to go in. Maybe it was aimed a little too high, or perhaps hit too hard. But, and this is important, *it had a chance!*

TECHNIQUE:

Once again, set up for a perfectly straight stroke to a breaking putt. But rather than aiming to make it, consciously aim higher, above the hole.

CONCEPT:

By consciously trying to miss high, you'll eventually eliminate ever hitting it low. You'll always give yourself a chance.

DRILL:

Find a breaking putt on a practice green. From different distances, read the break, set up for a straight putt, and roll the ball so that if it misses, it rolls by on the pro side, above the hole. (Don't cheat, keeping it high by stroking too hard: The ball should never finish more than 17 inches past the hole.) You also might do this drill with one of the straight-stroke devices mentioned on page 69.

The Pro (High) Side

The Amateur (Low) Side

TIP: The subtle message here is that to get above the hole means playing more break than you think is there. Do this regularly and you'll begin to play for more break automatically.

The Amazing Truth About Putting

The previous two sections show that most amateurs miss below the hole and underread break. Obviously there is something wrong with the way golfers read greens. A few years ago, Dave Pelz studied how golfers read and stroke breaking putts. What he learned, his "amazing truth," is that golfers make two serious mistakes. First, they drastically underread break, by as much as four times. Second, they try to correct their bad reads by making subconscious manipulations in their alignment and stroke to steer the ball back to the hole. That means everything about how they handle breaking putts—the read, the alignment, the stroke, and the result—is bad.

In conducting his tests, Pelz had hundreds of amateurs (and pros) read a putt and tell him how much break they saw. He knew how much it really broke and, incredibly, the average read was only 25 percent of the actual break: If the true break was four feet, they read it as one foot.

Without revealing their mistake in the read, Pelz had the same golfers set up over the same putt. His measurements showed they were aiming at a spot about 65 percent of the way to the true break, or about 32 inches high on that four-foot (48-inch) breaker. See figure 3.8.

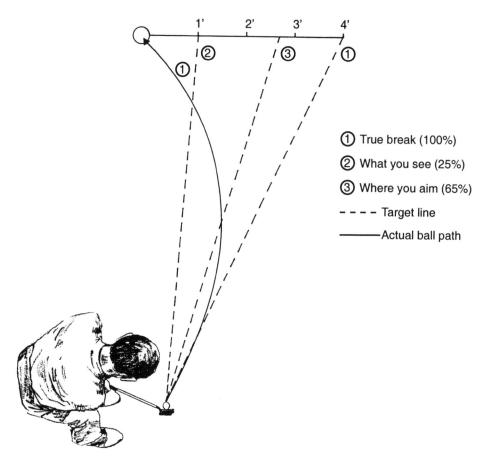

Figure 3.8

Then they were asked to stroke the putt. What Pelz saw was subconscious movements of the arms, hands, and club that steered the ball a little higher, a little closer to the true break, to a point 85 percent of the way there, about 41 inches. But even with all that, the ball still finished seven inches below the hole. (These numbers are averages: Some golfers did better, some worse, and that included tour pros and teaching pros, who generally did slightly better but still didn't read the real break.) See figure 3.9.

Not seeing enough break has two serious effects. First, and most obvious, the putt still misses below the hole because the manipulations aren't enough. But it also destroys golfers' hopes of making a straight stroke. Without realizing it, most golfers are steering their putts toward the hole, subconsciously manipulating the arms and hands. They're swinging in-to-out and out-to-in across the target line, making different compensating moves with every putt. No two strokes are alike, but none are straight-back and straight-through. As a result, they don't know what a good motion feels like or how to produce it.

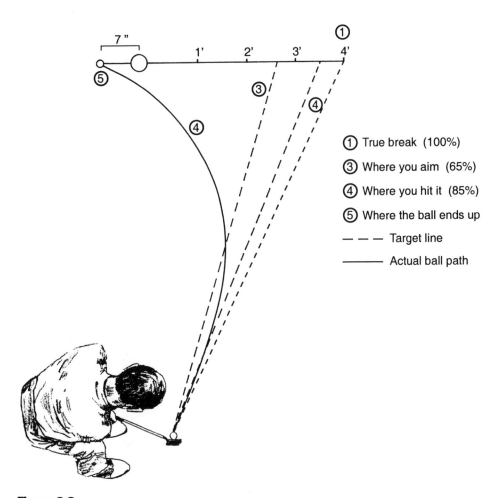

Figure 3.9

Solving the Amazing Truth

There is no quick fix for years of subconscious manipulation. But over time, you can improve your green-reading and fix your stroke.

Play more break. Starting with the very next breaking putt you encounter, *double* your read: If you see one foot of break, play two feet of break.

Learn to make a straight stroke, free of manipulation. Putt under a string and watch the putterhead go straight-back, straight-through. Go back to the chapter on the stroke and work on the fundamentals outlined there: Use a putting track or lay two clubs on the ground. Groove a straight stroke until you make it every time, on every putt. See figure 3.10.

As you work on your green-reading and stroke, your putting will improve. Since your mind isn't being forced to make a manipulating stroke, it will begin to see more of the real break. In time, your putts will miss

Figure 3.10

consistently on the high side. That means you're reading too much break and it's time to lessen the read, increasing it by only 75 percent; you can read even less when those miss consistently above the hole.

But it will take some time to clear your subconscious and ingrain a good stroke; until then, double your "read" and practice a straight stroke.

The "Triple Threat" drill, which follows, helps you solve this "Amazing Truth."

13 Triple Threat

STRATEGY:

Once you understand the effect of the "Amazing Truth," you know even more than ever that the key to making breaking putts is a straight stroke.

TECHNIQUE:

Find a sloping part of the practice green when there is one hole that allows you to make a left-to-right, a right-to-left, and a straight uphill putt, each in the 12- to 15-foot range (it's not hard; if a putt breaks one way, it's going to break the other way from the other side and probably have an uphill element as well). You need six pencils and three pieces of string, creating straight-stroke lines for each of the three putts described. Your lines for the two breaking putts should be aimed like this: Read the breaks, double what you see, and add two inches. (So if on the right-to-left putt you "see" it breaking 12 inches, set the line at a spot 26 inches above the hole.) The three lines should intersect at a point beyond the hole. Make the strings high enough off the ground that you can fit your putterhead beneath. Finally, on the two breaking putts, stick a tee in the ground about half an inch above the strings, on the "high" side of each putt, about four feet from the ball.

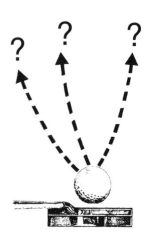

CONCEPT:

Dave Pelz designed this drill to ingrain the "Amazing Truth" and show that a straight putt, hit to the right spot, will find the hole. It also proves that we drastically underread breaking putts. If you make a straight stroke and the ball is still rolling below the hole, reset the line higher: It means your initial view of the break is very far off.

DRILL:

Take your address with the ball and putterhead under the string, your eyes directly over them. Using the line to help you make a straight stroke, hit three balls from each spot, following a consistent order (e.g., three left breakers, three right breakers, three straight). Repeat the same order. Never hit more than three balls in a row from one spot.

On the breaking putts, the ball should pass just below the tee stuck in the ground, then find the hole. If the ball hits the tee or passes on the high side, you are still making stroke compensations. As with all putts, the speed should be enough that misses finish no more than 17 inches past the hole.

TIP: Nothing will improve your putting like learning to consistently make a straight stroke. But nothing is harder than learning to make a straight stroke on breaking putts. This drill, although complicated, speaks to nearly every important concept in putting—a straight stroke, proper speed, and the right break. You should do it as often as you can, and continue even after you see your green-reading skills improve.

Plumb-Bobbing

You've probably seen pros on television, or perhaps someone in your weekend foursome, standing on a green, dangling the putter in front of his face, squinting, and looking at the hole (figure 3.11). This is "plumb-bobbing," a technique many golfers swear helps determine how a putt will break. Plumb-bobbing can tell you how the ground slopes under your feet; but it won't say much about the break near the hole, which makes it less reliable on long putts. It also gives only a general sense of the break, not its severity.

Stand so your eyes, the ball, and the hole are on line. Then set your body so your eyes, shoulders, hips, and knees are parallel to the ground beneath you. Stand comfortably, feet spread apart, and look at the hole.

Extend your arm straight out, holding the putter grip lightly between your thumb and forefinger so the club hangs freely. Sighting with one eye, raise or lower your arm until the bottom of the putter shaft covers the ball. Without moving your head, look up at the hole: If it is to the right of the shaft, the slope is left to right; if the hole appears to the left of the shaft, the slope is right to left. If the shaft is covering the hole, the putt is straight.

© Sam Greenwood

Figure 3.11

Final Thoughts About Breaking Putts

When reading greens, most golfers spend too much time figuring out where to aim and not enough wondering how hard to hit the ball. Speed and slope are interdependent. The amount of break is affected by the ball's speed: Hit it hard and break is minimized; roll it softly and the break is more prevalent.

If you prefer charging the hole, you'll learn over time to play less break. If you are a die putter, letting the ball just topple in, more break will make you more successful. If you don't have a preference, practice both ways and see which is more comfortable and effective.

The best help on breaking putts is experience. But there's no reason some of it can't come from the other golfers in your group. Watch their putts roll and break and factor that information into your reckoning.

Lastly, don't spend too much time reading a putt. If you look long enough, you're sure to see something— probably break that really isn't there. Your first impression is usually the best, so take a look, don't waste time, and make a good stroke.

Tiered Greens

There is good news and bad news about putting on two-tiered greens, putting surfaces with two levels, one higher than the other. The bad news is that if the hole is on the higher level (figure 3.12), your ball inevitably finds its way to the lower level, meaning you have to putt up the hill; conversely, if the hole is cut below, your ball finishes above, so you have to worry about the speed coming down the slope as well as break. The good news is that the levels usually are pretty flat, so you only have to deal with the slope that joins them. Here are two rules to remember for handling tiered greens.

From higher to lower. The ball will break toward the lowest point of the green, so aim well above the hole. Your bigger problem is speed, so imagine a hole cut on the target line an inch in front of the slope. Try to die your putt at this new hole so it is almost stopped when it catches the hill and begins picking up speed.

From lower to higher. The ball will slope away from you and toward the edge of the green. And because the ball is rolling uphill, the break will be sharper than it looks; aim higher above the hole. Finally, make a strong stroke, being sure to get the ball up the slope and onto the upper shelf.

Fringe Putting

Most greens are surrounded by a collar of grass that is longer, and shaggier, than the putting surface. If your shot into the green is a little short

Figure 3.12

or long, the ball may stop in or against this fringe, presenting you with a less than perfect lie (figure 3.13). There are a few different ways to hit a perfect shot out.

In the fringe. When the ball sits in the longer grass, the obvious choice is to chip. But unless you are a superior chipper, remember the golden rule of play around the greens: "A bad putt is better than a bad chip." A putt is better because it is easier to judge the speed of a rolling ball than a flying one; a putt is more accurate than a chip; and most players are more aggressive putting than chipping. So putt whenever you can.

If the ball is sitting up in the fringe grass or the fringe isn't too long, use a putter, taking your normal grip and address. The important choice is whether or not to sole the club: The center of the putterface should be level with the center of the ball, so you might hover the club slightly over the blades to assure clean, crisp contact, as in figure 3.14. (This also keeps the head from snagging in the grass on the takeaway and through-stroke.) Make a level stroke, contacting the middle of the ball.

Figure 3.13

Figure 3.14

Don't hit under or down on the ball; both will get the ball hopping instead of rolling, launching it well off-line.

If your ball has settled down in the grass, try a derivation of the chiputt explained in the long putting section on page 57. Position the ball well back in your stance, in-line with or even behind your back foot. Hold your putter with your putting grip, tilt your hands well ahead of the ball, pick the club up quickly, and drop it on the back of the ball, as seen in figures 3.15a and 3.15b. The ball will pop up and come out hot, making it a good play when there's lots of green to cover; when you're close to the pin, expect a lengthy come-backer. The drill on pages 86–87, "The Fringe Pop," helps you judge how hard to stroke your putt from the fringe.

a   b

Figure 3.15

© GolfStock

The Great Putters
Arnold Palmer

There was, and is, no mistaking Arnold Palmer on the golf course. He's the one lunging into the ball, hitching up his pants, and leading the biggest gallery. It was true 40 years ago and remains true today.

In that 40 years, he won four Masters, two British Opens, one U.S. Open, and another 75 or so other events worldwide. But more important than the wins was the man himself, for Palmer transformed the game when he burst onto the scene in the mid-1950s. His go-for-broke style of play excited the fans, and he was the obvious leading man for the television age, when the box brought golf into millions of homes.

Palmer's boldness extended to the greens. It's unlikely any ball he ever stroked died in the hole. He banged everything to the back of the cup, and if he missed, even by several feet, he'd set up and bang it home from there. No problem.

His technique was a combination of the orthodox and the original. His eyes were positioned over the ball; his grip was a reverse-overlap, which allowed the hands to work as a single unit (although the stroke was a little wristy); and despite his devil-may-care attitude, the stroke remained low to the ground and smooth. What was different was the stance: He pinched his knees together, turned his feet in until he stood pigeon-toed, and bent deeply at the knees and hips, hunching over the ball. These adjustments locked him into position, keeping him absolutely still throughout the stroke.

There was no arguing with Arnie's prowess on the greens. It's unlikely anyone holed as many cross-country birdie putts. He was especially good under pressure, emphasis on the "was." As he aged, the putting went first. He experimented with different makes, models, and styles of putters (he owns hundreds) and even tinkered with technique (but never straightened up his stance). By the time he reached the Senior Tour, he was as erratic on the greens as most older men.

It didn't matter. Win or lose, Arnie was playing the game he loves and having fun. And the whole world was right there with him, loving every minute of it, too.

14 The Fringe "Pop"

SITUATION: You have a hard time judging how hard to stroke putts from the fringe around the green.

STRATEGY:

First, putting is almost always better than chipping. But how you putt depends on the quality of the lie. The point of this drill is to try both methods of putting and see which gives the best results from a number of fringe situations.

TECHNIQUE:

It varies depending on the lie.

If the ball is sitting on top of the grass, you can use your normal putting stance and grip. Try beginning with the putter both soled lightly atop the grass and hovering slightly so the middle of the putterhead is directly behind the middle of the ball.

If the ball is down in the grass (and this is when the drill becomes especially educational), position the ball back in your stance: The farther down it sits in the grass, the farther

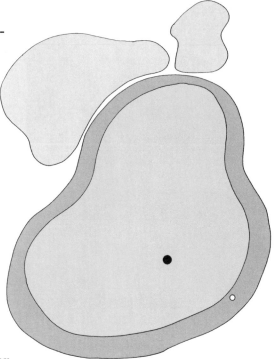

back in your stance it goes. Be careful, when placing the putterhead behind the ball, not to disturb the lie and move the ball; that's a penalty.

CONCEPT:

It's trial-and-error. You have to see for yourself how the ball reacts from different lies. And it's going to do so differently at different golf courses, based on the kind of grass and its length. So it's smart to make a few practice fringe putts every time you play at a new course.

DRILL:

Drop four or five balls into the fringe, use the techniques described above (depending on how far down into the grass the balls drop), and make your stroke: Use your putting

14

grip, angle your hands and the clubshaft well ahead of the ball, pick the club up quickly (you may want to hinge the wrists), then drop it steeply onto the back of the ball, "popping" it out of its lie.

Be sure to carefully place a few balls on top of the grass, sitting up as if on a tee, and use your normal putting address and stroke. Practice addressing with the putterhead touching the grass and hovering, and see how those react: Starting with the club lower should loft the ball more, which might be good when the hole is close to you; if it's far away on the green, the hover method, which will produce more overspin for more roll, might make sense.

> **TIP:** It's very difficult, no matter how the ball lies in the grass, to control distance. But be sure you hit it hard enough that the ball gets out of the grass and onto the green. Don't get cute, try to finesse the putt, and face a second fringe putt from only a few feet closer. You'd rather face a long putt from on the green than another one from deep among the long stuff.

Against the collar. When your ball has rolled up against the collar of fringe, the easiest way to putt isn't with the putter but with a wedge (figure 3.16). Grip your sand wedge as if it were a putter, aligning the leading edge with the middle of the ball and square to your target line. Without soling the club, make your normal putting stroke. This is a shot to practice before you take to the course; also try it with a few different wedges to see which produces the straightest, most controllable roll.

If the fringe grass is so long and thick that you can't line up the wedge with the ball, "kick" it with the toe. No, not on your foot, but the toe of your putter. See figure 3.17. Turn the putter 90 degrees in your hands so the toe of the club is pointing down the target line. Aim carefully for contact dead center on the ball, letting the club slice through the grass with minimal resistance. Choke well down the club, onto the shaft if necessary, play the ball off your front foot, focus your eyes on the back of the ball, and take some practice strokes first to get a feel for the club cutting through the grass. You'll probably find this shot most effective on short putts; the longer the backswing, the worse your chances of good contact. The following drill, "The Collar Wedge," demonstrates the skill and art of getting through long fringe grass.

Figure 3.16

Figure 3.17

15 The Collar Wedge

STRATEGY:

It's almost impossible to use a putter here and have any control. You'd have to make a steep swing, and the putterhead probably will get snagged in the collar grass.

TECHNIQUE:

Putt with your sand wedge. Use your normal putting address and grip, and set up square to your target line. Don't sole the club, but align the leading edge of the face with the equator of the ball.

CONCEPT:

The wedge's rounded bottom lets it slip easily through the long grass, and if you can keep the leading edge properly aimed, the ball will roll straight.

DRILL:

Drop some balls so they are up against the collar of long grass. Using the sand wedge as described above, make a low, straight-back, straight-through stroke, making contact at the ball's equator. Watch for how much stroke produces how much roll, as well as being aware of any snagging of the club in the long grass. When you first try this, don't worry about a hole; just worry about technique. As it feels comfortable, try "putting" toward holes at different distances.

The Collar Wedge

15

TIP: It may be a wedge in your hands, but you're using it like a putter. Resist the temptation to set up as if for a chip, with your hands ahead and more crouched over than when you putt. Tell yourself, "It's just a funny-looking putter," and be very careful to use your normal putting stroke.

Chapter 4

Conditions

Now that you know how to stroke a putt and figure in the effect of the greens, your work is done, right? Unfortunately not. Golf is an outdoor game, played on a living, growing tract of land. And Mother Nature loves to have her fun.

Not all grass is alike. Depending on your location, you could encounter a lush putting carpet or a sparse weed patch. Obviously, the texture, density, and length of the grass will alter a putt's progress.

Believe it or not, golfers don't only play when the sun is shining and the breezes are still. Just as when driving a car or sailing a boat, rain and wind change how you have to think when putting a golf ball.

And lastly, you will encounter a condition created by man, one that few golfers know about but is responsible for thousands of missed putts—even the short ones—every day. It's called the "lumpy doughnut," but it is no treat.

Grass

In this country, you're likely to be putting on one of two types of grass: bent or Bermuda. Bent is a cool-weather grass, found throughout the northern part of the United States, where it won't be subjected to prolonged stretches of heat and humidity. Bent has soft, fine blades that grow close together to create a carpet-like feel and texture.

Bermuda is a warm-weather strain, a stronger, weedy-looking grass that can tolerate the sultry conditions of the southern states. Bermuda blades are longer, broader, shaggier, and sparser; rather than a lush carpet, golfers say Bermuda looks, and plays, like a wild shag rug, with the ball rising and falling in and out of the blades. Their different looks and feels give Bermuda and bent very different playing characteristics.

A golf ball will roll truer on bent greens, where break will be caused primarily by the contour of the land. On Bermuda, the ball will be affected by the uneven growing pattern of the grass itself. The principal component to watch for, and figure into your green-reading, is grain, the direction of growth. All grass has grain—blades usually grow toward the sun, toward water, and away from mountains—but grain is more pronounced in the longer, tougher, sparser Bermuda. Many "snowbirds" coming from northern states to the South in winter have a tough time adjusting to grain, something they don't have to deal with at home; they miss putts on warm-weather greens because they don't factor in grain's effects. Conversely, golfers visiting up north from the South expect more side-to-side movement on the greens but are fooled by bent grass's lack of grain.

The following rules about grain apply strongly on Bermuda grains, less so on bent:

1. Rolling into the grain, a ball will roll slower and shorter.
2. Rolling with the grain, a ball will roll faster and farther.
3. When grain runs the same direction as the break, the ball will move faster and more severely down the slope.
4. When grain runs against the break, the ball won't break as fast or as far.

The practice green is a good place to check for grain and its effects. Find a straight putt and see how it really rolls. If it breaks significantly, you could be looking at strong grain, which you then will have to factor into your calculations of a putt's distance and direction.

Checking for Grain

There are two simple ways to "see" grain. One is in the color of the grass; the other is around the hole.

Stand behind your ball looking toward the hole. If you are looking downgrain (so you'll be putting in the same direction that the blades are growing), the grass will appear light and shiny. If you're hitting into grain, the blades growing toward you, they will look dark and dull. If you can't see a change in appearance, walk 90 degrees to the side, perpendicular to your target line, and look at the grass again; from this angle, you should be able to tell from the color if your putt will be breaking with or against the grain.

You also can drag your putter on the grass in the direction your putt will be rolling. If the blades pop up, you're heading into the grain; if they stay close to the surface, it's downgrain. This is a good way to practice your grain-reading efficiency, but it's a rules violation to do the putter-drag test during a round.

Now look at the hole and how the grass around it is growing. The way it was cut by the mower can tell you a great deal about grain: If full blades of grass are growing in toward the hole, that's the downgrain direction; on the upgrain side, the grass will be short, shaggy, and roughly cut from the morning mowing.

Grain changes during the day, usually becoming stronger as the grass grows. And in the South, where Bermuda grass can grow quickly, particularly on a hot, wet day, just a few hours' difference can make grain stronger.

Windy Putting

A gentle breeze shouldn't have much effect on a putt. However, once the winds pick up, they can influence a rolling ball's speed and ability to take the break. Therefore, the suggestions that follow only count when the wind is strong; don't drive yourself crazy factoring in all sorts of extra movement from light winds.

When the wind is strong and blowing in the same direction your putt will roll, not only can you stroke the ball more softly, but you should play a little more break. (The same is true when hitting a full shot with the wind, which exaggerates any sidespin.)

When the wind is blowing into your putt, naturally you have to hit it harder. Besides making a longer stroke, try to make pure contact so the ball rolls end over end, boring into the wind like a knockdown approach with a mid-iron. A head wind also minimizes break, straightening out a rolling ball. (Since a firmer stroke lessens the severity of any break, the combination of the two could eliminate sideward movement entirely. It's a matter of feel and experience.)

The effects of a side wind are obvious: more break when blowing in the same direction that the land slopes (or with the grain); less break when blowing against the slope and/or grain. When figuring in a side wind, don't forget it also will change a putt's pace, speeding up a ball moving the same way, slowing it when they are in opposition. And when the putt will be rolling faster, break will be multiplied yet again; a wind-slowed putt will break less.

Besides thinking how the wind will move the ball, think what it will do to you. Sudden gusts or a sustained gale can throw off your balance, which is crucial to good putting. You should be able to feel when your center of gravity is too high and the wind is causing you to tense your legs and back in an attempt to stand still. Rather than building tension, widen your stance and, if necessary, bend further over at the hips to create a more stable base. You'll have to choke down on the putter to compensate, which reduces the power transmitted from the club to the ball, so make a slightly more powerful stroke.

Putting When Wet

Water on the greens usually means putts will roll slower and straighter, so stroke the ball more firmly and expect less break. Should the green become saturated, it's not uncommon to see a ball refuse to move altogether, even when hit hard. Water creates great resistance and adds weight to the ball. (It also can be harmful to the green to walk and play on it when there's standing water. That's when it's probably smarter to pack it in, dry off, and plan to come back another day.)

The exception to the rule about water is dew. This thin layer of moisture can make a ball roll faster (if it rolls at all; it's more of a skid) and take more break. Be aware of this if you play early in the morning when the first few holes are coated in dew and putt faster; once the dew burns off, the later holes may roll very differently.

The "Lumpy Doughnut"

One "condition" caused not by the weather but by the golfers who played on the green before you is something that Dave Pelz has labeled the lumpy doughnut. It's what happens to the area right around the hole (see figure 4.1), and it can play nasty tricks on even a well-struck putt.

Start with some numbers. An average foursome of golfers leaves about 500 footprints on a green. It takes more than two hours for a footprint to "heal," the compacted grass rebounding back to full length. But in that time, thousands more footprints are made, so the grass and soil is trampled, squished, and flattened almost everywhere on the green—except right around the hole. Golfers are extra careful not to step within about a foot of the cup, so a two-foot-wide circle around the hole is

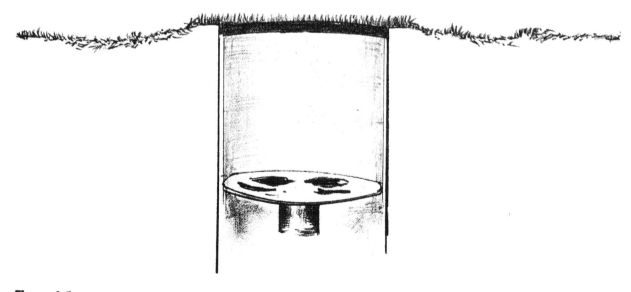

Figure 4.1

untouched and raised slightly above the rest of the green. (This is true for every group but the very first one out in the morning.) This circle, with the hole in the middle, is Pelz's lumpy doughnut.

A ball rolling toward the hole has a great deal of trouble to negotiate: Besides footprints, spike marks, and other man-made hazards on a green, there are also the natural break, bad spots in the grass, unrepaired ball marks, and the like. Now say it survives all that. As it is making its final approach to the hole, rolling at its slowest speed, the ball suddenly encounters the "lumpy doughnut," literally a ramp of untrodden turf: It doesn't have enough speed to handle this rise, so it rolls off it to the side. A perfectly struck putt, one that would have fallen into the hole had the surface been level all the way to the cup, has been deflected. Not by much but enough to make it miss.

You can't do much to eliminate the lumpy-doughnut effect: As long as golfers putt to the hole, walk over to it, tap in, and fish the ball out, the doughnut will exist. The way to handle it, says Pelz, who conducted extensive research, is to stroke your putts with enough speed so that if they were to roll directly over the hole and not fall in, they would roll 17 inches past. This speed, he found, is perfect for handling the ramp around the hole: The putt rolls straight but isn't going too fast to keep it from dropping in. (There's more on the 17-inch rule in chapter 2.)

The next drill, "Make Waves," is designed to help your putting in wet situations. The drill after that, "The 17-Inch Rule," describes Dave Pelz's technique mentioned earlier.

16 Make Waves

SITUATION: Dew or rain on the green causes havoc with your distance control.

STRATEGY:

Early in the morning or after a rain, the greens are going to be wet. While a little bit of water might make the ball "skid" and roll a little farther and faster, a little more and your putts will be slowed, sometimes significantly. If you choose to keep playing rather than heading into the clubhouse, you must know how to handle wet greens.

TECHNIQUE:

Take your normal address position, but you might try these alterations:
• Do whatever you can to get a little more power from your stroke. Try holding higher on the grip (but be sure to stand a little taller to compensate).
• Move the ball around in your stance. Playing it forward might get it more on top of the water when it starts moving; playing it back will create a crisper blow, but you might lose any advantage if the ball begins by moving down, deeper into the wet.
• Make a longer backstroke for more power.

CONCEPT:

Raymond Floyd actually goes out after a heavy rain and looks for spots where the water has pooled. He puts on his rain suit, drops some balls in the puddle, and practices different shots (especially chips and pitches) to see how the ball will react. He knows that water makes things different. The same applies on the greens, which will rarely get so soaked that water pools up, but are often slick, especially first thing in the morning. You've got to have a feel for what wet greens do to the ball.

DRILL:

When the dew is on the ground or after a rain, get onto a practice green (checking with the pro first to be sure it's open) and putt four or five balls to different hole locations. Look for breaking putts (both ways), up- and downhillers, different grain conditions, whatever variety you can.

TIP: If you're the first one on a dewy green, use the moisture to tell you something about how putts break. Find some sloping putts, make your best read, then give it your all and try to sink the breakers using a straight stroke. Besides looking for the final result, look at the trail the ball makes through the dew. Sometimes it takes this visual image to get across the idea that break is bigger than we think.

The 17-Inch Rule

> **SITUATION:** Almost every putting situation except for severe downhills and very short putts.

STRATEGY:

Dave Pelz proved scientifically that the putts with the best chance of handling the lumpy doughnut and finding the hole are those hit hard enough to roll 17 inches past the cup.

TECHNIQUE:

The "17-inch rule" applies no matter what type of address, grip, or putter you use. It has nothing to do with your technique, everything to do with the ground beneath your feet. So use your normal putting technique (if you make any allowances, your results won't be consistent or helpful). The only thing not to use is a hole: You want to see the ball roll past, not fall in. Use a coin as your target.

CONCEPT:

Most putters are perfectly happy just to find the hole. It almost goes against logic to hit the ball harder than that, trying to roll it nearly a foot and a half past. Your test won't be as scientifically accurate as Pelz's, but it should help convince you that he's right.

DRILL:

Place a coin, preferably something large and shiny like a quarter or half-dollar so you can see it easily, on the putting green. Starting from a variety of different positions and lengths, putt three or four balls from each spot, trying to make the ball roll directly over the coin and stop 17 inches past (which is about half the length of your standard-length putter). You can stick a tee in the ground 17 inches behind the coin if that helps you get a better feel for the distance. Feel how hard you have to hit it, probably slightly harder than you would be stroking it for the same distance, to roll it past. Think about that feeling whenever you putt.

TIP: A little aggression, say 17 inches' worth, will help on just about every putt you'll face for the rest of your golf career. Okay, maybe not on the tap-ins and the slick downhillers, but for breaking putts, uphill putts, straight putts, and into-the-grain putts, that extra effort is the same as trying to accelerate. And now that you know what the lumpy doughnut is and how it's caused, be extra careful when walking on the greens not to leave extra-deep footprints or step too close to the hole. You wouldn't do that, would you?

The Great Putters
Billy Casper

After Billy Casper won the 1959 U.S. Open, played over the tight and treacherous Winged Foot Golf Club north of New York City, Ben Hogan supposedly said to the new champion, "If you couldn't putt, you'd be outside the ropes selling hot dogs." Indeed, Casper's swing appeared better suited to a short-order cook than a major championship winner: Left arm straight an unnaturally long time both back and through, wrists firm, stance open, ball well forward. Odd-looking, but effective.

Yet not as effective as his putting stroke. In his prime, from the late 1950s into the early '70s, and again in the early days of the Senior Tour, Casper was, without question, one of the game's great putters. At the '59 Open, he needed only 112 putts over four days. He won a second U.S. Open in 1966, beating Arnold Palmer in a playoff. Casper also won the 1970 Masters, after finishing second the year before, and poor putters simply don't succeed on the slick, undulating greens of Augusta National.

The Casper method employed as little motion and exertion as possible, relying almost exclusively on the hinging of the wrists. With the ball well forward in his stance and the club held with a relaxed, reverse-overlap grip, nothing moved but the hands and the putterhead. In Casper's words, "each hand has a separate role to play": The right provided the power, snapping the club into the ball as it approached impact; the left held the clubface square to the target while resisting the desire of the right hand to roll over. The result was a "rap," a short backswing followed by a longer finish (although the follow-through shortened on shorter putts).

Casper maintained that wristy putting was easier to repeat than the firm-wristed method. That may be true for professionals who can devote hours to practice, grooving the proper amount of wrist snap. However, most pros, and certainly most amateurs, who don't have the hours necessary to work on stroke and feel, disagreed both then and now. But for Billy Casper, and for a good long time, it worked.

© UPI/Corbis-Bettmann

Chapter 5

Equipment

How to Choose a Putter

You're in the market for a new putter, so you walk into your pro shop or an off-course golf store, head to the rack of magic wands (figure 5.1), and which one do you pick up? Probably the one that your friend, a

Figure 5.1

good putter, uses, or the one the hot tour pro endorses, or one that looks nice. Congratulations! You've just used three of the worst criteria to make one of the most important equipment decisions in the game.

A putter has definite specifications and characteristics that can have either a very good or very bad effect on your putting prowess. Here, in order of importance, are the qualities to look for when buying a putter. (Thanks, once again, to Dave Pelz for his insight in matching players to putters.)

Shaft Length and Lie Angle

The shaft length and lie angle (figure 5.2) must fit your physique and posture in three ways.

- Most important, the shaft length and lie angle (the angle of the shaft coming out of the head) must let you stand at address with your eyes directly over your target line and your hands under your shoulders.

Figure 5.2

- The shaft must be long enough that you can practice for a long time without pain in your back, lower legs, shoulders, etc.
- The shaft must be short enough that it won't catch in a sweater, rain gear, or other clothing.

Error Compensation

You want a design that helps eliminate your most common mistakes. To determine what that is, take the putter you use now, stick a piece of impact tape (available at most golf stores) on the face or dust the face with talcum powder, and stroke 30 putts. The marks on the tape or in the powder will indicate where the ball meets the putterface, as in figure 5.3. If it's generally toward the heel, you want a heel-shafted putter (the shaft enters the head near the heel so the sweetspot is closer to that end). If you tend to make contact toward the toe, look for a center-shafted putter (the shaft enters the head away from the heel and more toward the middle, which is where the sweetspot will be).

Figure 5.3

Alignment Aids

Lines, arrows, and other markings on the crown or top line of a putter, as seen in figure 5.4, are legal under the rules of golf. Use them! Anything that helps you make a straight stroke and flush contact should be encouraged.

Weight Equals Touch

That's the weight of the clubhead. Find a putter with a very light clubhead and stroke some putts with it. Then tape a few dimes to the back or sole and try putting again. Does that feel better or worse? Are your results better or worse? Try a number of different putters, being conscious of head weight, and find the one that produces the best touch for you.

Grip Size and Shape

The size of the grip should be small enough to allow you good control, but large enough that the fingers don't overlap one another uncomfortably. As for shape, the putter is the only club on which it is legal to have a flat-faced grip. This flat area on the top side makes it easier to place your hands consistently; the same if there are edges or corners you can feel. Find a grip that encourages taking hold the same way time after time. (If the putter you like doesn't come with such a grip, you can choose from hundreds of putter handles that can be installed in minutes.) See figures 5.5a-c for a look at grips small (5.5a) and large (5.5b).

Figure 5.4

a

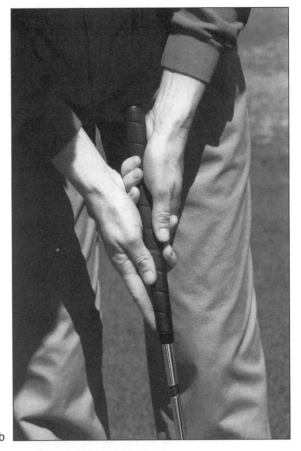

b

c

Figure 5.5

Feel vs. Forgiveness

The most forgiving putters have extra weight in the heel and toe areas so putts hit away from the sweetspot still produce good results in distance and direction. But due to their design, most forgiving putters provide less feel. Which is more important to you? Forgiveness or feel? Try some heel-toe-weighted putters and some less forgiving designs (mallet heads, blades, and so on). See figure 5.6. Do you care about the sensation of impact? Do you make contact all over the face? (Impact tape or talcum powder on the face will help determine that.) You must choose between good feel and good, equipment-provided results. Sometimes you can find a shape that produces some of both.

How NOT to Choose a Putter

Don't worry too much about the following:

- Appearance: Yes, it should look good. But any putter that drops the ball into the hole will start looking good real fast.

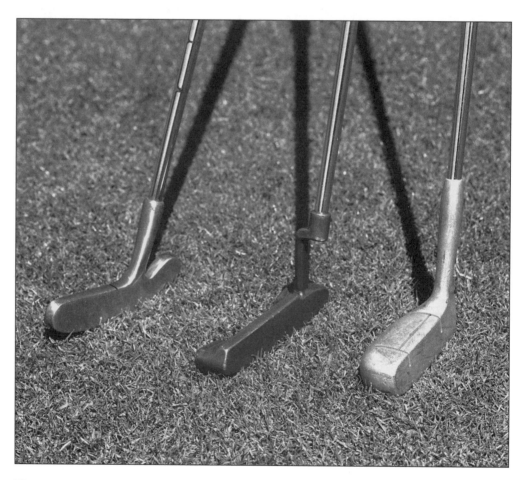

Figure 5.6

- Sound at impact: If it gives you confidence to hear a particular sound, great. If not, don't worry.

- Professional endorsements: The pros choose on the basis of the considerations listed above. So should you, and how they relate to your game.

- What your friends use: It's one thing if you try your friend's putter and instantly begin holing everything in sight. But Harry probably is a great putter because he found a flatstick that fits him properly.

- Price: The dumbest reason of all. If you take the time and make the effort to pick a putter that suits you, it could be the last one you ever buy. How much money will you save then?

Find, and Use, the Sweetspot

Every golf club has a sweetspot. It's that area of the face that produces pure impact, impact that feels good, looks good, and has the best results. When you flush a drive or smooth an iron, what you are feeling is the ball being struck on the sweetspot.

In actuality, the sweetspot is a small area around the club's center of gravity, and when it is struck, the clubface does not twist. When the face twists, as it does whenever contact is made away from the sweetspot, the club no longer points at the target (assuming you were aiming that way to begin with), you feel the vibrations, and shots start off-line. But catch it in the sweetspot and the ball goes right where you were aiming and the feel is indeed sweet.

Putters have a sweetspot, too, and although it isn't very large, it isn't hard to hit if you set up properly and make a good stroke. How important is hitting the sweetspot to good putting? It is the third, and statistically most important, of Dave Pelz's three ingredients of putting success. According to his research, 95 percent of the error associated with missing the sweetspot is transferred to the ball. How much is that? Miss the sweetspot by one-quarter of an inch and you'll miss every putt longer than eight feet.

The sweetspot on a putter often is marked by a line or arrow cut into the topline, that part of the putter you can see as you're standing at address. But very often the mark is inaccurate: Not by very much, but as you now know, even a tiny error is enough to have significant effect on distance and direction. So even if your putter already carries a manufacturer's indicator, you would be wise to locate the sweetspot yourself and mark it properly.

How to Find the Sweetspot
With your thumb and forefinger, pinch the end of the putter grip very lightly so it dangles straight out in front of your body and can swing

easily. Do *not* hold it straight up and down, but angle it slightly to approximate the slant of the shaft when you are putting (tilt the shaft until the sole of the putterhead is parallel to the ground).

Using the eraser end of a pencil, the tip of a tee, or some other small point, tap the putterface lightly so it swings back and forth, as in figure 5.7. As you tap, watch how the face reacts and feel what's happening. Keep tapping until you find a spot that sends the head swinging back and forth without any twisting of the face, without wobbling, and with little to no vibration. That is the sweetspot.

Mark the sweetspot on the face (keep checking to be sure you're right on it), then scratch a small groove into the topline directly above it. You might want to fill the groove with white paint so it's easy to see when you address the ball.

Loft and Putting

Back in the 1920s, Bobby Jones used a hickory-shafted putter nicknamed "Calamity Jane." He won all his big tournaments with it, and after he retired, it was mass-produced and thousands sold to amateurs.

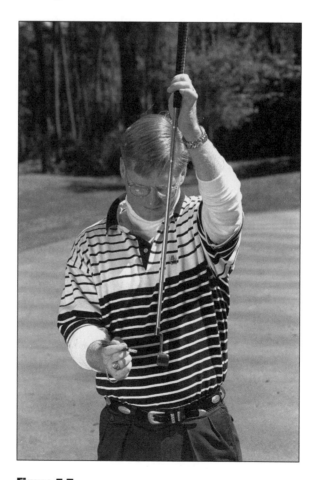

Figure 5.7

One feature of Calamity Jane was loft: The face was angled about 14 degrees back from vertical. As a result, Jones's putts were lifted off the ground when he hit them, a necessity in an era when even the best greens were inconsistent in grass length and condition. Jones wanted to keep his ball as high as possible atop the blades of grass; if it settled down into the ragged areas, there was no telling how the ball would react or where it would finish.

Today, with better greens and more consistent equipment manufacturing, most putters carry only a few degrees of loft. A little loft is necessary so the ball isn't driven into the turf at impact: That would cause it to pop up and roll off-line rather than stay on the intended path. A little bit of loft also looks more pleasing to the eye at address.

If you're putting on longer, shaggy greens, still a little more loft may be helpful, as it was in Jones's day. Create loft by moving the ball slightly forward in your stance, toward your front foot: You'll catch it on the upswing, lifting it slightly off the ground for the first few inches. Conversely, you might want to move the ball slightly back in your stance on tightly mowed, fast greens, to encourage crisp contact and good roll. Make a few practice putts before a round to check the greens' conditions.

You also might move the ball forward in your stance if you think it's taking too long to get rolling after impact. That may sound strange, but a ball doesn't begin rolling as soon as it's hit. For the first few inches the ball actually skids until friction slows it down and roll takes over. Dave Pelz measured the amount of skid at a fairly consistent 20 percent of a putt's total length. He said that although there is nothing the golfer can do to prevent skidding, it can be used to one's advantage if made as smooth as possible, without any bouncing or hopping. To do this, be sure impact is made with a little bit of loft on the putter, either built into the face or created by moving the ball forward. See figures 5.8a–c.

Unsure about your loft at impact? Set up in front of a full-length mirror and watch as you make some normal strokes. Do you make a forward press, pushing the hands toward the target, before your stroke? Or is the shaft leaning toward the target coming into impact? Both of these actions deloft the putterface and could be affecting your scoring. Experiment with less forward press or a more vertical shaft position (try moving the ball forward in your stance) and see if that helps.

If the ball is too far forward and the shaft actually leans *away* from the target, some shifting at address could keep your putts closer to the ground and, in the end, put them closer to the hole.

The Long Putter

A few years after the Senior Tour got rolling in the early 1980s, a number of the older pros began using an over-long putter (figure 5.9). It was

a

Hands forward, less loft.

b

Hands centered, normal loft.

c

Hands back, more loft.

Figure 5.8

© Sam Greenwood

Figure 5.9

invented by one of their own, Charlie Owens, who, like many older golfers, was afflicted with the "yips," a loss of control over the putting nerves. Owens' solution was to stick a second shaft into an existing putter, creating a new wand more than 50 inches long (most putters are 34 to 36 inches). As a result, he stood much taller at address, giving him a good view of the target line.

Owens experimented with different ways to hold the extra-long shaft, splitting his hands more than a foot apart. He anchored the top of the club against his breastbone with his left hand (the lead hand when putting the conventional way) and swung the long putter like a pendulum with the right hand. Owens became competitive again, and very soon many of his Senior fellows adopted his invention. A number of long-putter companies were formed, and for a few years it wasn't uncommon to see the long sticks among weekend golfers as well as on television with the Seniors.

Long putters have lost some of their popularity, although a few players still use them on the tours. They claim that not only does it cure the yips, it also eliminates breaking down of the left (leading) wrist, a common cause of missed putts with a normal-length putter.

18 Long-Putter Practice

STRATEGY:

You've read it before, but it's worth repeating: Putting accounts for nearly 43 percent of the game, yet we use only one club for all putts, regardless of their length. The other 57 percent of the game is handled by the other 13 clubs, with the choice determined by the length of the shot. So maybe you should change putters for different-length putts?

TECHNIQUE:

The technique for using a long putter is described in the text. Warm up a little with it first, then conduct the drill as outlined below. When using your normal-length putter, use your normal technique of grip, address, stroke, and so on.

CONCEPT:

Just because the long putter seems to have lost favor among the pros doesn't mean it can't help you. Dave Pelz's testing with students of all skill levels finds that the long putter is more effective on short putts (those inside five feet) than a standard-length putter; conversely, the standard-length putter makes more putts, and leads to fewer three-putts, than the long putter outside 20 feet.

DRILL:

Roll 12 putts on a practice green: four from inside five feet, four from 15 feet, and four from outside 30 feet (try to find equal numbers of up- and downhillers, left- and right-breakers). Using one ball and only one try, putt all 12 with your long putter and then all 12 with the standard-length putter. If you have time, reverse the order of the putters and repeat the test. Do this three times on three different days in one week, and keep note of the results. If your own tests show you make more short putts with the long putter, why not carry two putters? You'll probably use the other putter more often, and more effectively, than that hard-to-hit 3-iron in your bag.

TIP: Pelz's long-putter/normal-putter test actually had a third element, and that was using the normal model with the left-hand low grip (explained in Chapter 1). The full results of his test were:

- From inside five feet, the long putter was most effective, followed by left-hand-low. Normal-putter/normal grip was last.

- From outside 20 feet, the normal-length putter was most effective, followed by left-hand-low, with the long putter last.

What's the point? If you still don't want to carry two putters, try using just the normal-length one, but change your grip on those distances, long or short, that bother you the most.

It takes a little practice, but you won't find a purer pendulum putting method anywhere: By holding the top of the putter firmly against the sternum, the shaft swings exactly like a pendulum, with the other hand merely drawing it back and letting go. So if you're uncomfortable crouching over the ball, have wrist-breakdown problems, or just want to incorporate a true pendulum stroke, the long putter is a viable alternative.

Using a Long Putter

Turn your left hand upside down (thumb up), wrap it around the end of the club, and anchor it against the middle of your chest, as shown in figure 5.10. The right (lower) hand will take hold 12 to 16 inches lower—exactly how far is personal choice, based on comfort and results. Most long putters have two grips, one above the other, which will help position the lower hand.

There are many ways to hold on with the right hand (figures 5.11a and 5.11b). Slip the shaft between the fore and middle fingers; wrap the hand around it; hold on with the last three fingers, pressing the tip of the forefinger and thumb against the back side of the shaft. Whatever you do, don't grip too tightly, because you want gravity to determine the

Figure 5.10

a

b

Figure 5.11

putter's swing speed. The right hand should draw it back the proper length and then hang on as the putter swings through.

Stand as tall as possible. There should be a little bending at your waist and knees for balance, your feet spread shoulder-width apart. If you aren't comfortable in a perfectly square stance, open your hips and shoulders slightly; this clears a path for the swinging of the shaft.

The ball is positioned directly under your sternum, with contact made at the very bottom of your swing arc. And just as in conventional putting, position your eyes over the ball or the target line: If they're outside the line, you'll take the putter out to in; eyes inside promote an inside-to-out stroke. Remember: It's a pendulum, with the best results coming when it swings straight back and straight through with no encumbrances. See figures 5.12a–c.

The consensus among most golfers is that the long putter works best for short putts and not as well for long putts, which require a longer, harder-to-control stroke. If short putts are your problem, consider carrying two putters: one of normal length for most putts and a long putter for the short ones. It may seem a bit radical, but putting is 43 percent of the game, certainly important enough to warrant a second club if it helps you find the hole more often.

a   b   c

Figure 5.12

© GolfStock/Pete Marovich

The Great Putters
Jack Nicklaus

Jack Nicklaus made his mark on the game primarily from tee to green: Booming drives that flew past his rivals' best efforts; high approach shots that stopped dead by the pin; laser-tracking 1-irons that caromed off the flagstick. But he also was a solid, dependable putter, bringing the same intensity and thoroughness to his green play that he did to every other part of the game.

His accomplishments are legendary: six Masters, five PGA Championships, four U.S. Opens, three British Opens, two U.S. Amateurs, countless records for scoring, money, and whatever else the game has to offer. Like his long-time adversary Arnold Palmer, Nicklaus changed the game forever. When *GOLF* Magazine picked the "Player of the Century" in 1988, there was no choice other than the Golden Bear.

And like a bear, he stalked every putt, scoping it out from all possible angles. He seemed to be staring the ball into the hole. Only after analyzing all the factors did he settle into his trademark crouch, deep bend at the knees, stance open, palms and clubface aiming down the target line, ball forward, and then turn his head slightly so he could see down the line from the ball to the hole. His stroke was a little arms-and-shoulders, a slight hinging of the wrists, and, following a tip he learned upon first joining the tour, the right hand pushing the putterhead squarely down the target line.

Years later, the images remain vivid: Nicklaus rolling in a 40-footer on Augusta's 16th hole to snatch the 1975 Masters from Tom Weiskopf and Johnny Miller; the 22-foot birdie on Baltusrol's 17th green to deny Isao Aoki a chance at the 1980 U.S. Open; and, long after most of the world had given him up for dead, the arm-and-putter salute (capped by the big smile) after the 10-foot birdie on 17 that locked up the '86 Masters for the "Olden Bear" of 46.

Basking in the glow of what would prove to be his final major, Nicklaus said, "I really don't understand putting. I can't explain it." But he could do it.

Chapter 6

Practice

If you are seriously interested in improving on the greens, you're in luck. Putting is one of the easiest parts of the game to practice: You don't need a driving range, you don't need a sand trap, and you don't need much room at all. All you do need is a putter, a few balls, and a relatively flat surface like a bare floor or a carpeted room. It's something you can do when you have a few minutes in the office (although it helps if your boss is a golfer), before going to bed, or, my personal favorite, while watching the pros battle for the big bucks on television.

If you are practicing indoors, spend a few minutes before each session checking your set-up position in front of a full-length mirror. From the straight-on view (shoulders parallel to the mirror), look for your head position over the ball, the angle of the putter shaft, ball position between the feet, and the pureness of the pendulum stroke (no wrist break). See figure 6.1. Turning perpendicular so you're putting toward the mirror, swivel your head (don't lift it) and look for your eye position over the target line/ball, hands directly under the shoulders, knee and hip flex, and the putter's lie angle relative to your comfort level. If you can, make some practice strokes in this position, trying to watch if the putterhead swings inside, outside, or remains directly over the target line on all but the longest swings.

Indoor practicing is also a good time to lay two clubs down on the carpet, as in figure 6.2, and work on a straight-back, straight-through stroke without a ball. Or if there's a straight-line pattern on your carpet or floor, use that to check the putterhead's movement back and forth. Drop a coin on the carpet and try to roll a ball over it and 17 inches past. You also might putt with your eyes closed, compete with yourself, roll

Figure 6.1

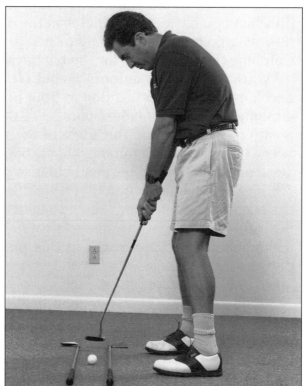

Figure 6.2

25 in a row to the same spot, the same things you'd do outdoors on the practice green.

Of course, it's unlikely you'll ever encounter greens as bumpy as even the flattest carpet or as fast as a hardwood floor (figure 6.3). But these exaggerated surfaces can help you develop better touch, learn to contact the sweetspot, make an accelerating stroke, ingrain a pre-stroke routine, eliminate wrist break . . . and on and on and on. Practice is not only rolling the ball into a cup.

Always make at least a few practice putts before starting a round. Get the putter in your hands for a minute or two and stroke a few short ones and a few long ones. Get a feel for the speed of the greens and the day's tendencies: Are you tending to push or pull your putts? Better to find out before that miss on the first green. Finish up by rolling in two or three three-footers, because nothing better prepares you to play well than hearing the plop of the ball hitting the bottom of the cup.

Be competitive. Get a friend, or putt with two balls, and make it a contest with the loser buying drinks. Pressure is a great teacher.

A few minutes every day for a few weeks will lead to noticeable improvement. Any of the following practice drills, as well as the ones mentioned in previous chapters and ones you might think up yourself, will help. The following drills will help you in your putting practice.

Figure 6.3

19 Right Hand Only

SITUATION: You lose the feel for how hard to hit your putts.

STRATEGY:

Each hand has a different function in putting. The right hand is usually the "power" hand, because it's lower on the grip, in a more powerful position. When your distance control is shaky, take your left hand off the putter and practice with just the right.

TECHNIQUE:

Set up as you normally would, positioning the ball in its normal spot, your head directly over it, and so on. Then remove your left hand from the grip. Maintaining a light grip, and letting the putter swing slightly inside going back and after impact, hit 10 to 20 putts.

CONCEPT:

Forget direction! You want to think distance here, and the right hand's capacity for making the right amount of stroke.

DRILL:

Set up as described above and putt to a hole, a tee stuck in the ground, a coin, anything. Don't worry about the line, but feel how hard and how much you moved the right hand to propel the ball the proper distance. Don't think about the putterhead; concentrate on the right hand, the lightness of its hold, and its range of motion.

TIP: This tip wasn't invented by Jim McLean, but I've borrowed it from him because of something he says: "Many tour pros use [this drill] when preparing to putt on unfamiliar greens." In other words, it's a great way to test the speed of greens at a new course; it's especially good if you begin by not putting to a hole, but simply getting the feel for how much stroke produces how much roll.

20 Left Hand Only

STRATEGY:

It only makes sense that if the right hand is the power hand, the left is the "control," guiding the putterface back and through.

TECHNIQUE:

Set up normally. Remove your right hand from the grip. Maintaining a light grip, and letting the putter swing slightly inside going back and after impact, hit 10 to 20 putts.

CONCEPT:

By concentrating on the left hand, you can see two things: what happens to the putterface, which should remain perpendicular to the target line throughout the stroke, and what happens to the left wrist, which should remain firm without breaking down.

DRILL:

Set up as described above and putt a series of two-footers to a hole. Make sure the left hand accelerates through impact with the wrist remaining firm (no hinging!). As your success rate climbs, move back to three feet, then five, then 10.

20

TIP: Jim McLean notes that this drill strengthens your left hand and forearm, further helping improve your control. Think of the back of the hand as being parallel to the putterface, so swinging the hand toward the target will result in good direction.

21 Watch the Dot

SITUATION: You're having problems making a good, smooth stroke.

STRATEGY:

Some golfers can't close their eyes and putt, so they have to look somewhere. But sometimes the worst place to look is at the putterhead and the ball, since that encourages worrying about contact. A dot on the grip gives you somewhere else to look and can encourage a better stroke.

TECHNIQUE:

Take paint or white typewriter correction fluid and put a small dot at the bottom of the grip on the front side. You want to be able to see it when you've taken your normal address position. Without moving your head, watch the dot move from the address position to the top of the stroke, through impact, and to the finish. Don't do anything different other than where you look during the stroke.

CONCEPT:

Johnny Miller gets credit for this drill, but he actually used it in competition and won the 1976 British Open with his putter so doctored. It was easier to make a fluid stroke since he wasn't worried about anything except the movement of the dot. That allowed him to make a stroke with the ball getting in the way of the putterhead's motion; he didn't think about impact, he simply let it happen.

DRILL:

Try putting five balls with your normal technique, watching the ball and the putterhead, then try it staring at the dot. You should feel the second five putts are smoother and made with less tension. Concentrate on the dot as well as watch it; get your mind off the quality and impact and the result. Think dot!

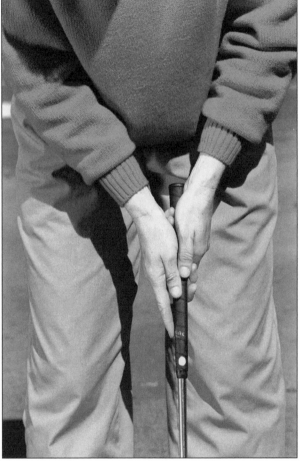

TIP: If you don't want to mark your putter, find something else to stare at: your thumbnail, a logo on the putter shaft, your wristwatch. Keep your focus well above the ball and you'll make a better stroke naturally and unconsciously.

22 Steady the Head

SITUATION: Your head tends to move during the stroke.

STRATEGY:

By using something other than a putter, you are forced to concentrate harder on impact.

TECHNIQUE:

Set up for your normal putting stroke, but use your sand or pitching wedge (whichever has the straighter leading edge) rather than the putter. Hover the clubhead slightly off the ground so the leading edge will strike the very center of the ball.

CONCEPT:

Jim McLean says this drill actually has three advantages: 1) It forces you to keep your head steady for good impact; 2) it helps develop hand-eye coordination; and 3) it forces you to concentrate.

DRILL:

Start by making a series of three-footers. Watch for the quality of the roll (end over end), as well as both distance and direction. Once the three-footers are rolling in, move back to five feet, then 10 feet.

TIP: Once you're good with the short putts, move back to the long ones, 20 feet or more (and really good doesn't mean holing out but rolling them consistently close for a tap-in second putt). Then go back to using your putter and be amazed how pure your stroke has become.

23 A Ball in the Hand

SITUATION: You're losing feel by exerting too much tension in the hands and arms during the stroke.

STRATEGY:

It's like saying "whatever you do, don't think about a hippopotamus." Now it's hippo, hippo, hippo. The same with tension: When you're consciously trying to do away with tension, you can't help but squeeze the grip tighter and constrict the muscles of the upper body. Here's a way to relax without really trying to.

TECHNIQUE:

Holding the putter with your normal grip, slip a golf ball between the shaft and the last two fingers of your left (higher) hand.

CONCEPT:

This drill was used by Walter Hagen, the master showman/golfer of the 1920s and '30s, who was one of the greatest short-game players of his or any time. He knew tension was a crippler, but said this drill put more of the hand's pressure into the remaining fingers, which smoothed his stroke.

DRILL:

With the ball between the fingers and the shaft, make a few practice putts. After four or five, drop the ball and try to replicate the smooth stroke and relaxed feeling with your normal grip.

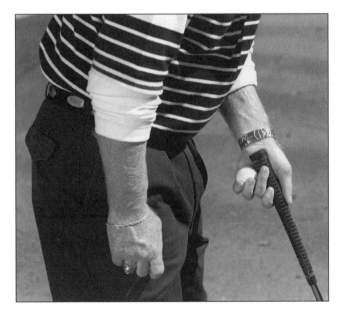

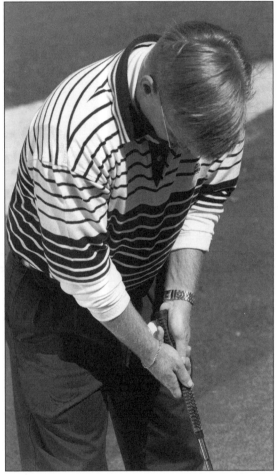

TIP: Hagen said putting this way would unlock the smooth, natural stroke inside every golfer. It's an especially good drill to use in situations extra-heavy in tension: long putts, downhillers, and breakers.

24 **Drawback**

SITUATION: You want to sharpen your skills and become more aggressive.

STRATEGY:

There are hundreds of putting games you can play that will help you improve. But simply putting head-to-head against someone doesn't put enough pressure on you. This does.

TECHNIQUE:

The game is called "Drawback," and while there are many variations and ways you can play, the basic tenet is that you imagine a 17-inch half-circle behind the hole (you can mark it with string or tees). When practicing putting, either against an opponent or by yourself, you must either hole the ball or make it finish inside this half-circle. If it finishes either long or short, you must draw the ball back the length of your putter. So if you finish three inches short, your next putt is from 38 inches away.

CONCEPT:

This is a Dave Pelz game, one he's been using for years to show just how important it is to get the ball to the hole. It encourages living by the 17-inch rule as well as being aggressive.

DRILL:

Use one ball and create a putting challenge for yourself or with friends. Mark the 17-inch half-circle behind a series of holes and play the circuit as a competition. Remember, if you're short of the hole or too long (past 17 inches), move the ball 35 inches farther away.

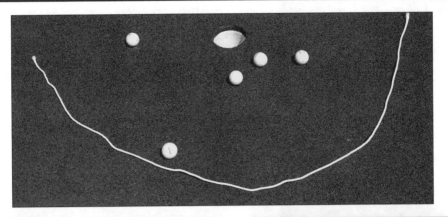

TIP: One variation is to move the ball two putter-lengths away if you're short of the hole, emphasizing how stupid it is to not get it there. Facing a six-foot second putt is a good way to learn to make a better first putt.

© GolfStock/Keiichi Sato

The Great Putters
Ben Crenshaw

Ask golf fans to name the greatest putter today, and most will say Ben Crenshaw. "Gentle Ben," one of the kindest, most soft-spoken men you'll ever meet, is indeed a wizard with the flat stick. Although he hasn't won as often as some tour veterans still out there (19 wins in 25 years as a pro), Crenshaw owns two green jackets, the kind that can only be picked up in Augusta, Georgia. Both Masters victories, in 1984 and 1995, were won in large part thanks to a syrupy putting stroke and almost uncanny ability to read greens for speed and direction.

Crenshaw's stroke is as smooth as you'll ever see. He never rushes, matching the rhythm of his work to his naturally laid-back personality. Standing tall and slightly open to the target, he makes a stroke that moves like a full swing, starting low to the ground, then turning to the inside in sync with the rotation of the shoulders. Because he doesn't make any manipulations to keep the clubface over the target line, it rolls open on the backswing and rolls closed at the finish: The secret to Crenshaw's success is the ability to make contact when the face has returned to square. That's touch, grooved through years of practice.

The long, languid motion continues past impact, gliding to a stop well after the ball is on its way. It is putting poetry in motion, and it never varies.

Something else that never changes is Crenshaw's choice of weapons. As a boy, Ben received a blade-style putter from his father. He still uses that model, having long ago adapted to its idiosyncrasies. (It's an old-fashioned design, very low-tech, demanding impact on the sweetspot for control of distance and direction.) A few years ago, one of the putters was stolen from Ben's bag after a tournament. He offered a reward and eventually it was returned. Of course, he has others just like it at home, but that's not the point.

The inside-square-inside stroke can be very difficult for amateurs to master unless they have hours to devote to practice. But after watching Crenshaw execute it to perfection time after time, even the highest handicapper will be tempted to give it a try.

Chapter 7

Mental Focus

The mind plays an important role in determining the success of every golf shot. But it seems to have an especially strong effect on putting, where everything is smaller—the stroke, the clubface, the target—and so demands greater focus. That's why it's not unusual to hear players say they "willed" a putt into the hole, awarding their psyches telekinetic power: One hears it so often on the golf course that it's tempting to think there is some truth to it.

Use Your Head

Actually, there is. The mind does hole a lot of putts, exercising its power in a number of different ways.

First, your brain must see the path you want the ball to take to the hole. By ingraining the line somewhere between your ears, your body will find a way to make it happen. You may not even realize it, but as Dave Pelz proved when measuring how golfers read and play break, the body subconsciously compensates, changing the stroke to meet the brain's demands. So you want to have a good mental picture of the line and speed of every putt.

The mind is also the seat of the putter's greatest weapon: confidence. Put another way, if you think you are a good putter, you probably are (or soon will be). Thinking positive thoughts keeps the negative ones away. There will be no room in your head for "Should I charge it or lag it?" or "Maybe it's an inch more to the left." Your last thought should be an unhesitating "Get it to the hole!" or "Hit it to the right edge of the cup!"

Nearly 80 years ago, Jerome Travers, one of the great early American golfers (and putters) said, "In the game of golf, confidence is a great helper. Let a player lose it and he is marked for slaughter." More recently, Raymond Floyd, one of our great modern champions, summed up the essence of confidence in putting when he wrote, "Remember, you're a good putter. Don't ever forget it."

The "Yips"

You're standing over your putt, addressing the ball, comfortable, ready to take the club back, when "Boom": The putter goes off in your hands. With an uncontrollable spasm, the hands and wrists have taken violent action, firing the ball well past (or left, or right, or short) of the hole. You didn't mean to do it. It wasn't really a stroke. You're not sure what happened.

It was a "yip."

Many famous players have suffered with the yips, often in their later years. Ben Hogan, Arnold Palmer, Tom Watson, and Sam Snead (who may have first coined the term) have battled them. The long-term effects can be career-ending. At the very least, they've driven otherwise confident golfers to develop strange grips, pose in bizarre stances, use weird clubs (the long putter was designed to defeat the yips), and take a drink before, after, and even during a round.

One school of thought thinks the yips are mental, something having to do with a loss of nerve. Johnny Miller, who recently came out of a retirement begun partly as a way to escape the yips, says, "It's a mental thing with me. When I sign my name, sometimes the pen jumps and there's nothing I can do. There's a loose wire back there or something."

Loose wire or tight nerves, there is no sure cure for the yips. But the first thing the yipper must do is make a change. Of what? Anything. Try a new putter, a new grip, a new stance. Look at the hole instead of the ball, or close your eyes and look at nothing at all. Start the stroke when you breathe in rather than when you breathe out. Hum a song. Play for a spot a foot short of the hole. It almost doesn't matter what you do as long as you do something different. It's time to take a new route, shake up the system (mental or physical, doesn't matter), and see if a little shock will turn things right.

Sometimes you'll see a pattern. If the left wrist breaking down is the culprit, switch to a left-hand-low grip that makes it harder to hinge. If your hands don't feel in control, squeeze the grip so tightly your knuckles turn white. If your body lurches with the stroke, widen your stance enough to make lateral movement impossible.

There's one side effect of the yips almost every sufferer reports: Once you've had them, you live in fear they will return. Here's where a positive mental outlook can help. Convince yourself that you can make a smooth, solid stroke. Think aggressively. And if the occasional bad stroke sneaks in, don't dwell on it; let it go, forget it, move on.

A Radical Solution to the Yips

During the 1966 PGA Championship, a 54-year-old Sam Snead twitched so violently on a putt that he actually struck the ball twice on the same stroke. He knew what was happening and the only way he could think to stop was to make a radical change that would calm his nerves. That's when he turned his putting stance 90 degrees, setting up over the ball as if he were playing croquet, his left hand gripping the very top of the putter, the right hand more than halfway down the shaft, and holed his first putts on the next three greens. He was using his arms like pistons, totally eliminating any wrist action, and it was working.

The USGA soon declared Snead's method illegal because he was straddling the line, a violation of golf's rules. So he made a little change, bringing his feet closer together on the same side of the line. His body still faced the hole like the putter, and the end of the grip was slightly more to the side, but he was still holding the top steady and moving only the lower hand back and forth directly above the target line. It became known as putting "side-saddle." (See figure 7.1). This is such a drastic change from conventional putting (more so than switching to a long putter) that it just might work.

Side-saddle-style putting has a great deal to recommend it. The result is a nearly perfect pendulum stroke (anchored at the top), made with no wrist movement at all. For yippers, it has the advantage of changing nearly every aspect of normal putting: stance, orientation to the hole and target line, ball position, eye and head position, you name it. And, as Snead and a few others proved, it can work.

So should you use it? If the alternative is the yips, it might be worth a try.

Figure 7.1

25 Flex Your Forearms

SITUATION: You're fighting the yips.

STRATEGY:

Eliminate the touch from your putts by increasing the muscle tension in your forearms. George Low, who earned a reputation as golf's greatest putter in the 1960s and '70s by putting with his foot (and usually beating competitors using putters), came up with this remedy. He had only a mediocre career on tour but helped many struggling pros and amateurs with their putting. He said, "Everyone has had or will someday have the yips," a not-too-comforting thought.

TECHNIQUE:

Low thought the hands caused the yips, so his method was to take them out of the stroke by creating as much tension as possible in the forearms. He felt this would eliminate the chance of making a short, quick, jabbing stroke.

CONCEPT:

Like other putting theorists, Low was suggesting the yipper do something differently to clear his system of this spasmodic motion. Adding tension is one way to do it, but there are hundreds of others. Do whatever you can differently and see if that gets rid of the yips, even if only for a short time.

DRILL:

In Low's words, he tightened his forearms "as I would if I were showing off my muscles, and also crouch down a little more. With these changes, all I can do is shove the ball: hand action is practically eliminated." Stroke as many practice putts as necessary for you to feel that the yips are going away. Once you've "squeezed" them out, go back to your normal technique and see if they've been eradicated. If not, try again, or try something else.

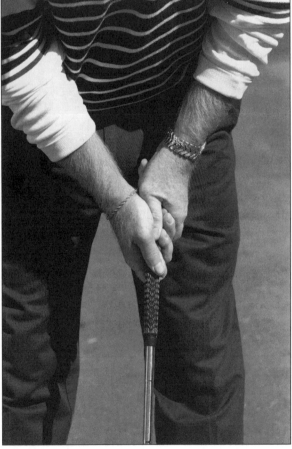

TIP: Low also thought the yips resulted from a fear of missing putts. To cure that, his suggestion was to hole a lot of putts in practice, rolling in the short ones over and over and over again until your stroke improves and your confidence level rises. As he said, "No fear, no yips."

The Great Putters

The Moderns

Golf nears the year 2000 healthier than ever: More players, more courses, bigger purses, and more talent on, and fighting to get on, the pro tours. And, it could be argued, more good putters, particularly in the pro ranks. Here are a few of the best right now.

© GolfStock/Pete Marovich

Brad Faxon

Faxon is proof of that overused adage, "Drive for show, putt for dough." He is regularly among the tour leaders in putting statistics, and among the laggards in driving. Wild off the tee, he is wonderful on the greens, which explains why he also is a leader in birdies. His great strength is the ability to clear his head: "Believe it or not," he says, "I'm not really thinking about anything when I putt. I let my instincts take over. When I'm putting well, I feel as if I can make everything." He changes his technique slightly on long putts, standing a little taller at address and letting the wrists hinge and even the head move during the stroke.

Jim Furyk

Better known for an odd, looping swing, Furyk is a highly skilled putter whose principal bit of unorthodoxy is a left-hand low (cross-handed) grip. Back in the 1970s, when Furyk was just beginning to play, his father asked Arnold Palmer and Gary Player what, if anything, they would do differently if they could start their careers over: Both said they'd putt left-hand-low. It's worked for the self-taught Furyk from the get-go.

Phil Mickelson

If you hold a mirror up to Ben Crenshaw, what you see is the left-handed Mickelson. Like Crenshaw, he makes a long, smooth stroke, which moves to the inside going back, is square at impact (producing pure sweetspot contact), and moves back to the inside in the follow-through. However, unlike Crenshaw, Mickelson has yet to prove himself a pressure putter, able to hole the big ones when they really matter.

© GolfStock/D. Darden

Nancy Lopez

After more than 20 years as a pro, nearly 50 tour titles, and a place in the LPGA Hall of Fame, can Lopez be considered "a modern"? Yes, because she's still winning and her stroke is still one of the best. However, it's really an old-fashioned motion, dependent on hinging of the wrists. And reminiscent of another wristy putter of bygone days, Billy Casper, Lopez says her wrist stroke is easy to learn, easy to repeat, and holds up under pressure.

So what's the consensus message from today's best putters? If it works, do it.

Trust your initial impression. Take a quick look at the hole and, without thinking, ask yourself which way it breaks. See it going a little left to right? Chances are it does. The longer you analyze slope, grain, shadows, spike marks, and the effect of the full moon on today's tides, the more likely you are to "see" break or something else that isn't there. Your instincts probably have gotten you pretty far in life: Let them help you on the course.

Lastly, be aggressive. Ben Crenshaw once said, "There are four ways to miss the hole: right, left, long, and short. If you always reach the hole, you eliminate one of those four ways." Or as Yogi Berra put it, "Ninety percent of all putts left short don't go in the hole." Or something like that. (Being aggressive also supports Pelz's 17-inch rule, rolling the ball a little harder to minimize the effect of on-green hazards.)

The bottom line is, if your mechanics are good but your mindset is poor, the putt has no chance. However, a good mind can overcome poor technique.

Chapter 8

Etiquette

You now know how to putt. But do you know how to act on the green? There are many rules in golf that you don't need to have memorized (that's what the rulebook is for, and you should have one in your golf bag at all times). But you do need to know, and observe, the many customs of good sportsmanship that make golf special. Here are the most important ones that apply on the green.

When someone else is putting, don't stand where he can see you or your shadow, don't make noise (jingling change in your pockets, tearing open the Velcro closure on your glove, "accidentally" coughing), and don't applaud his miss. It's okay to commiserate over a missed putt or congratulate a good one, but it is extremely rude to cheer a missed attempt even if it helps you or your team.

Always mark your ball. You can use a special ball mark; there's probably one attached to your golf glove, and they usually are given away in the pro shop. You also can use a coin, a rock, even a leaf as long as it's something you can identify and that won't move (a leaf probably isn't a good idea on a windy day). Place it directly behind your ball, on the extension of your target line (figure 8.1).

If your mark is on another player's line, ask if he wants it moved and to which side. Place the heel of your putter next to the mark and replace it just outside the toe. After the player is done, return your mark to its original position before replacing your ball; if you forget and putt from the new spot, it's a penalty.

Be careful where you walk on the green. Know where the balls of the other players are and don't walk on their line or the extension of their line on the far side of the hole. Always give the hole a wide berth (figure

Figure 8.1

Figure 8.2

8.2) until you either tap in your ball or pick it out of the cup.

When walking on the green, even safely out of everyone's line, don't drag your feet. That tears the grass, creating spike marks that cannot be repaired by a golfer lining up a putt. (Spike marks can be repaired only after you've finished putting.)

Watch what you say after holing out. A casual comment like, "Boy, that putt was faster than I thought," can throw off players who have yet to putt. It's illegal to give advice (except to your partner in a match), so a comment like that, even when dropped accidentally, could be considered a violation of the rules. Worse is when you intend to confuse another golfer: It's called "gamesmanship," and while it isn't illegal, it's unkind and will come back to haunt you when others refuse to play with you.

Finally, don't dawdle. You don't want to rush, but you shouldn't take too long. Watch the pros on television and you'll see many of the best take what seems like an eternity lining up a putt, checking it from all sides, plumb-bobbing, squatting and standing and walking around, then standing at address for what must be an uncomfortably long time to hold such a pose. Even though they are pros, playing for the big bucks, it's inconsiderate. Learn to make a quick read, doing most of your scouting while the other players are putting, being careful not to stand in their line or bother them in any other way. Then, as soon as it's your turn, step up to the ball, take your address, and stroke it.

While you can't fix spike marks, you can repair ball marks (also called "pitch marks"), the indentations made when a ball hits the green. Not only can you fix ball marks, you should: Look for the one you made, fix it, and fix one or two others (being sure to do so quickly).

Fixing a ball mark takes about 10 seconds. If you fix it the right way (described below), that spot on the green will heal in three to five days. But an unrepaired mark won't heal for 15 to 20 days. It's bad for the green and bad for the golfers who come along afterward and have their putts knocked off line by the mark or the raised turf around it. So be kind to yourself, your fellow golfers, and the golf course and fix ball marks.

The Golf Course Superintendents Association of America (the guys who care for courses) gives these directions for properly repairing ball marks.

1. Use a pronged ball-mark repair tool (available in most pro shops), knife, key, or tee.

2. Insert the tool at the edges of the mark, *not* in the middle of the depression. Figure 8.3a.

3. Bring the edges of the mark together with a gentle twisting motion. Don't lift the center. Try not to tear the grass. Figure 8.3b.

4. Smooth the surface with a club or bottom of your shoe. You're done when it's a surface that you would be happy putting over. Figure 8.3c.

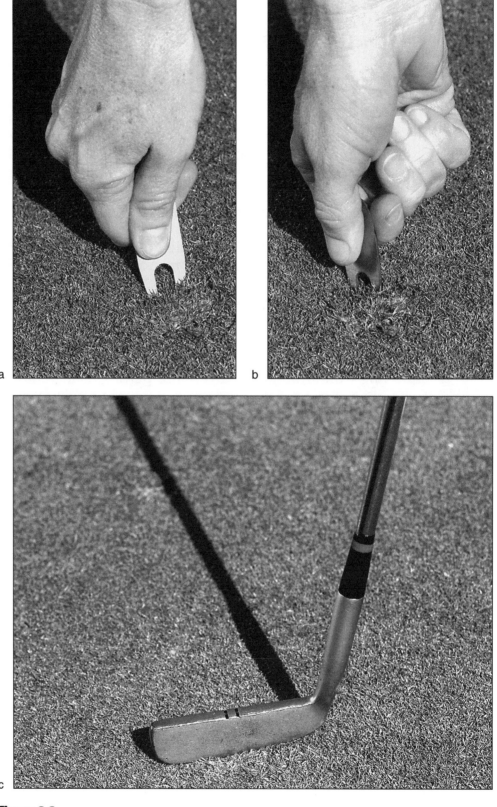

Figure 8.3

Index

About the Author

James A. Frank, the editor of *GOLF Magazine* since 1990, has become one of the foremost writers on golf instruction, especially regarding short-game skills.

Frank recently co-authored *GOLF Magazine's Complete Book of Golf Instruction*, for which he wrote the chapters on sand play, short game, and putting. He wrote the successful books *The Golfer's Companion* and *Golf Secrets* and co-authored several other books. He also authored a weekly series of golf tips for Gannett News Service for three years.

Frank lives just outside New York City. When he is not working or with his family, odds are great that Frank is inside 100 yards of the green.

The Precision Golf Series
From Human Kinetics

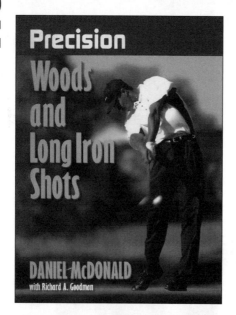

Add length and accuracy to your long game with this unique combination of on-course strategies and drills. Learn, improve, and then master tee shots, fairway woods, long irons, strategies for par 5s, and creative shotmaking.

Includes 58 long-game situations, 100 photos, and 68 illustrations to help you visualize the required shot and learn how to execute it. Fine-tune your club selection, swing technique, and course management for each long shot you face.

1998 • Paperback • 144 pp • Item PMCD0766
ISBN 0-88011-766-4 • $16.95 ($24.95 Canadian)

Take control of your short game. *Precision Wedge and Bunker Shots* will teach you to use creative shotmaking to turn problem situations into pars and routine situations into birdies.

Includes 53 short-game situations, more than 100 photographs, and 50 illustrations to help you visualize the required shot and learn how to execute it. Contains everything you need to improve your short game, covering club selection, correct technique, course management, and drills.

1998 • Paperback • 136 pp • Item PFIT0727
ISBN 0-88011-727-3 • $16.95 ($24.95 Canadian)

To request more information or to place
your order, U.S. customers call
toll-free 1-800-747-4457.

Customers outside the U.S. place your order
using the appropriate telephone number/address
shown in the front of this book.

HUMAN KINETICS
The Premier Publisher for Sports & Fitness
www.humankinetics.com